THE FAMILY VIRTUES GUIDE

The Family Virtues Guide is part of an initiative called The Virtues Project, whose vision is to empower adults and children in diverse cultures around the world to live by their highest values. It is not about the practices or beliefs of any one faith but is sourced in the virtues which are the common elements of spirituality found in all sacred traditions. The 52 virtues include:

- Caring
- Compassion
- Consideration
- Excellence
- Generosity
- Helpfulness
- Humility
- Justice
- Kindness
- Love
- Modesty
- Respect
- Self-discipline
- Tact
- Tolerance
- Trust
- Unity

THE FAMILY VIRTUES GUIDE

Simple Ways to Bring Out the Best in Our Children and Ourselves

Linda Kavelin Popov

with

Dan Popov, Ph.D., and John Kavelin

A PLUME BOOK

PLUME
Published by the Penguin Group
Penguin Books USA Inc., 375 Hudson Street, New York, New York 10014, U.S.A.
Penguin Books Ltd, 27 Wrights Lane, London W8 5TZ, England
Penguin Books Australia Ltd, Ringwood, Victoria, Australia
Penguin Books Canada Ltd, 10 Alcorn Avenue, Toronto, Ontario, Canada M4V 3B2
Penguin Books (N.Z.) Ltd, 182–190 Wairau Road, Auckland 10, New Zealand

Penguin Books Ltd, Registered Offices:
Harmondsworth, Middlesex, England

First published by Plume, an imprint of Dutton Signet,
a division of Penguin Books USA Inc.

First Printing, June, 1997
10 9 8 7 6 5 4 3 2

Illustrations by Joan Levitt Badke

The following terms have been trademarked: The Virtues Project,
The Art of Spiritual Companioning, Spiritual Companioning.

 REGISTERED TRADEMARK—MARCA REGISTRADA

LIBRARY OF CONGRESS CATALOGING-IN-PUBLICATION DATA:
Popov, Linda Kavelin.
The family virtues guide : simple ways to bring out the best in our
children and ourselves / Linda Kavelin Popov, with Dan Popov and John
Kavelin.
p.   cm.
ISBN 0-452-27810-4
1. Children—Conduct of life—Study and teaching.   2. Religious ethics—
Study and teaching.   3. Virtues—Study and teaching.   4. Moral
education.   5. Child rearing.   I. Popov, Dan.   II. Kavelin, John.
III. Title.
BJ1631.P67   1997
649'.7—dc21   96-53423
                                                                                        CIP

Printed in the United States of America
Set in Palatino

To the Angels of Virtue, especially Trust,
who gave us the strength to believe in the Project
and the will to bring it to life.

❧ CONTENTS ❧

❧ PREFACE ❧

Being a parent is the most complex and important activity on the planet. Parents are a child's first and most important educators, yet they receive little or no training in what to do or how to do it. Unfortunately, children don't come with instruction manuals.

There is a growing concern among conscientious parents that our children are caught up in materialism to the detriment of character, that they are picking up values which place personal gain before ethics, integrity, or love. Many of them have little or no sense of faith or spiritual values in their lives. What's a parent to do?

There have been valuable efforts to fill the void of parental guidance in recent years, efforts focused on seeing the child as a separate person with unique feelings and ideas. Much has been written about the emotional and psychological health of children and families, covering topics such as honoring a child's feelings, keeping peace in the family, building self-esteem, learning to speak so kids will listen, and learning to listen so kids will talk. What has yet to be addressed in a broad way is how parents can meet the spiritual needs of children.

The Family Virtues Guide is part of an initiative called The Virtues Project, whose mission is to provide multicultural programs and materials which empower people to remember who they really are and to live by their highest values. The project was honored during the International Year of the Family by the United Nations Secretariat and the World Conference of Cities and Corporations as a model global program for families of all cultures. The principles and practices in *The Family Virtues Guide* are being applied in families, schools, prisons, corporations, social-service programs, child-care centers, indigenous communities, and diverse faith communities throughout the world.

The Family Virtues Guide is not about family values. Values are culture-specific. It is about virtues, which are universally valued by all faiths and cultures in the world. Virtues are the silver thread running through all of humanity's sacred literature as well as the oral traditions of the world's indigenous peoples. Virtues are described as the qualities of the soul and the attributes of God. They are the means by which we can reflect the image and likeness of the Creator. They are also considered a very high order of angels.

The Family Virtues Guide is grounded in the sacred traditions of the world's religions, yet it does not promote the practices or beliefs of any particular faith. It is based on simple universal principles of spiritual growth. It views children as spiritual beings whose purpose in life is to have a life of purpose—to develop all the virtues they have within them in potential.

Although *The Family Virtues Guide* honors the various sacred traditions as the best source of our collective knowledge of virtues, it is designed to be helpful and accessible to all people, religious or not. It offers simple methods for paying attention to the spiritual and moral development of a child day-to-day. It is an approach to bringing out the best in every child, and in every member of the family.

Each day of living with children brings fresh opportunities for guiding them at "teachable moments" which pass quickly and may never come again. *The Family Virtues Guide* provides a framework and a language for making the most of these moments and helping children to set goals.

Parenting is made up of so many things—physical care, affection, encouragement, enjoyment, correction, protection—and teaching. Just as children's bodies need food, air, light, and warmth, their spirits need challenge, direction, and encouragement. *The Family Virtues Guide* is a tool to help parents consciously and skillfully address their children's spiritual needs so that they won't miss the precious opportunities which happen every day.

A key principle of *The Family Virtues Guide* is that parents are the first educators, those best able to impart values and virtues to their children. *The Family Virtues Guide* is a response to parents who want to bring simple spirituality and character education into their children's lives. The world needs people who are willing to take personal responsibility.

Let it be this generation.

Introduction: How to Use
The Family Virtues Guide

The Family Virtues Guide is based on four key principles:

1. The parent is the primary educator of the child.
2. Children are born in potential: their natural qualities can develop into positive or negative traits depending on how they are educated in the early years.
3. Character develops as children learn to make responsible, moral choices.
4. Self-esteem is a natural outcome of living by spiritual principles.

Naturally, you can't help someone else grow without growing yourself. Using *The Family Virtues Guide* is an inner adventure for the whole family.

The guide is a how-to manual for applying virtues in everyday life, for supporting each other to set spiritual goals. It is a guide to a simple language of spirituality—the virtues themselves. Some call it the language of the heart.

There are two sections in *The Family Virtues Guide*. The first contains three chapters about how to be a spiritual mentor to children, including suggestions in Chapter 3 for holding family meetings to focus on a virtue each week, if that is something which fits for your family. It is not essential to have a formal gathering of the family to apply the principles and practices in the guide. It is only one way to focus attention on the virtues. You will find that there are lots of small daily ways to apply the strategies in this book.

The second section of the book contains fifty-two virtues, one for each week of the year. It seemed somehow more manageable than including the more than three hundred virtues that we found in the world's sacred texts.

Each virtue begins with a small inspirational quotation from the holy book of one of the world's religions. Those included here are Hinduism, Judaism, Zoroastrianism, Buddhism, Christianity, Islam, and the Baha'i faith. (See References for sources used.)

Each virtue contains four pages:

Page 1. What is it?
Page 2. Why practice it?
Page 3. How do you practice it? and Exercises: "What would it look like if . . ."
Page 4. Signs of Success and a Daily Affirmation

Appendix A contains Group Exercises that you may find helpful in comparing notes with a friend or sharing with a small group to deepen your understanding of the practices in *The Family Virtues Guide*. Appendix B is an outline of the practical do's and don'ts of spiritual mentorship, from the first three chapters. Appendix C has instructions on how to make a virtues tree felt board. Appendix D contains information on The Virtues Project.

The Family Virtues Guide offers a simple moral structure which parents can model and within which children can build their character and self-esteem. It is no substitute for love, hugs, and family giggles, the joys of just being together. However, it is a tool for parents to use in guiding and teaching their children so that the content of their character is a first priority. It contains a language which can heal the hurts of one's own upbringing, because it supports parents in meeting the struggles of their own spiritual journeys with detachment and tenderness. It is a way to replace the internal critic with a gentle, vigilant observer. Many find that as they use this simple tool to parent their children, they are at the same time reparenting themselves.

We offer *The Family Virtues Guide* in a spirit of enthusiasm and confidence that you and your children will find it a valuable and enjoyable source of support in cultivating your virtues, the gifts within.

CHAPTER 1

Who Are Our Children, Really?

The Spiritual Nature of Children

"Virtue is the muscle tone that develops from daily and hourly training of a spiritual warrior." —TOLBERT MCCARROLL

A child is a spiritual being who is brought into the world to grow in body, mind, and spirit. A parent is a trustee, a guardian, a steward who is here to love and guide this new person, particularly in the early years. Inherently, children are learners. Research shows that their brains begin learning, actually processing information, even before birth. Parents are their first and most important teachers.

To teach children well is to bring out the best in them. Most of us have a vague idea of wanting the best for our children, from making sure that they have enough food, clothes, hugs, toys, and friends to giving them the best education we can afford. We want them to do well, marry well, and to have healthy children. We want to see them happy and successful. We wish them the best. What's best *for* them has everything to do with what is best *in* them. As one six-year-old girl said when asked what she thought virtues were, "Virtues are what's good about us." The virtues are gems in the mine of the true self. A parent is meant to mine a child's gems and bring them to light.

The Longing for Mastery and Meaning

We are born with a mysterious longing for mastery and for meaning. To keep learning, to keep stretching, to keep reaching for more. This is a deep spiritual need, a yearning of the soul which is often misinterpreted in the course of our lives as physical or material neediness. If only we had more popularity, more money, more love, more power, a better job, then we would be happy. Yet when we attempt to fill this longing by something physical or material, something external to the self, we remain unsatisfied. Sometimes we seek addictive ways to become numb to the pain of this longing, and we are left feeling even emptier, because only a connection to our spiritual purpose will truly fill the need. Some consider this purpose our connection with God. It is the call to realize our innate sense of wholeness and the move toward wholeness which is at the core of spiritual growth. Nothing else will give us genuine happiness.

What Kids Are

Like an acorn, which has within it the capacity to become a towering oak, a child has great potential. All children are born with all the virtues, the gifts within, waiting to grow. You may have noticed sometime or other a plant sprouting up through the concrete of a city street. The urge to growth is one of the strongest needs of any living thing.

What a child becomes is a result of four things: nature, nurturance, opportunity, and effort. Nature is a child's natural giftedness or virtues "profile." Although each child has all the virtues within them in potential to one degree or another, the potential for the development of certain virtues is greater in a particular child, just as a rose has different attributes than a chrysanthemum. Nurturance is how a child is educated, how his gifts are recognized and supported, the difference between watering a plant and letting it wilt. The opportunities children have to act on their virtues give them the possibility to become who they are. A great musician of world-class creativity without an instrument may never learn of the special music she has within her. Effort is a child's responsibility, his ability to respond to the opportunities to practice the virtues. Ultimately it is the choice of a child to act on her own potential. It is said that God provides nature and a parent provides nurture. The child himself must choose to respond to the opportunities in his life. Choice is at the core of moral will.

Authentic self-esteem and real happiness come naturally as children experience the emergence of their virtues. There is nothing more delightful than the look of love which comes over a baby's face, or the wonder and reverence experienced by a three-year-old examining a puddle or a leaf, the pride of purposefulness when children learn to tie their shoes or ride a bicycle, the deepening of confidence when they perform a small act of kindness or consideration. A child bringing you breakfast in bed, even if the toast is burnt and peanut butter is smeared onto an overflowing glass of chocolate milk (her idea of a deluxe breakfast!), brings a feeling of true fulfillment. "I made it myself, Mom!"

Adolescents are, by nature, fierce idealists, looking for a unique way to make a difference, an impact on the world. When idealism is thwarted, it becomes rebellion for the sake of rebellion, but when it is honored and supported, nothing can stop a young man or woman from passionate service. There are communities which have discovered this secret and have dramatically reduced youth crime by giving their young people opportunities to be of service in their own creative ways.

Virtue is sometimes associated with perfectionism. When it comes to human beings, to be perfect does not mean to be flawless. It means to be whole and complete. Part of the completeness of being spiritually alive and aware is to accept our flaws, our mistakes, and our failings as teachable opportunities which can bring us new learning. It is in working with the virtues which we have over- or underdeveloped that we find the energy for new growth. Life is not about being perfect. It is about perfecting or cultivating our virtues. Perfection is the process of bringing our gifts to fruition.

How can parents, grandparents, and caregivers support children to meet their spiritual needs for mastery and meaning? First, by seeing our children as the potential spiritual and moral champions that they are, beings with an incredibly deep sense of purpose. The Maori people of New Zealand have a practice of looking deep into someone's eyes and saying, "I see you." Seeing our children gives us the will to mentor them, to become good coaches. Rather than indulging them in physical or material ways or overprotecting them from their spiritual challenges, we become excellent at supporting excellence.

We have such a short but critical time in which to have a fundamental impact on the development of their character, which is the greatest asset for their happiness. Much of their character development is complete by the time they turn seven.

What Kids Are Not

We are used to thinking of children as psychological beings who need good physical care and also affection, respect, and a healthy balance between dependence and independence. The idea of a parent as a spiritual educator builds on yet goes beyond the notion of the child as a psychological being.

The Virtues Project offers a frame of reference in which a child's need for character education is primary. A parent, as spiritual mentor, focuses first of all on facilitating the child's moral readiness. In order to make the shift from caretaker to educator, it is helpful to let go of notions about children which are not true to their spiritual nature.

Your child is not born a blank slate upon which you will write. There is no such thing as a generic baby. True, a child's personality and character are not fully formed. But they are "in there." Just as an oak is in an acorn—not a spruce or a palm but an oak—each child is born with a special bundle of potential. In that bundle are three things:

- Inherited traits
- Individual temperament
- Innate capacities: gifts, talents, abilities, limitations, and virtues

Spiritual parenting involves a focus on a child's gifts and possibilities, a readiness to support them to develop all they can be—to give life their best effort.

A child is not a prince(ss) which parents warp into a frog. This is a modern notion which implies that if we left them to their own devices, children would be pure, undefiled, whole, and perfect. It contends that we are the ones who mess them up and "dethrone" them. This is a half truth. Parents do have enormous influence on children and can shape the script a child carries through life. But it is also true that left to their own devices, children are likely to take the path of least resistance, resorting to survival instincts, the animal side of their nature as material/spiritual beings. It is easier to develop the lower side of their nature, which doesn't require them to engage their will. So children very much need a guiding hand to lead them. They are not inherently "pure." They have the potential for both goodness and for destructiveness. Every quality they possess, every virtue, can be directed or misdirected. That's why your role is so vital to their success.

Your child is not just a reflection on you. This is a tough one to look at, since it is usually fraught with our unconscious needs. Your child is not living proof of your worth or shame. Your child is not here to prove anything. Life is not an art gallery. It is a workshop. Children who are used as approval objects for their parents have deep problems developing an authentic sense of self. An accomplished musician who attended a virtues workshop shared the horrendous pressure he felt as a child to be the "genius," to be the redeemer of his family. He has since wrestled with severe psychological problems. The very purpose of raising a child is to help her to become an independent spiritual being. There is your spiritual work and there is your children's. Part of your work is to support them in theirs.

It is really important for children's spiritual health that they not be treated as a little prince or princess (or a little frog, for that matter). It is one thing to acknowledge a child for having some special abilities. It is another to crow to the world and hold him up as a sign of your worthiness. This is not helpful to children, since what they need is the humility to keep growing no matter how wondrous their past achievements. Also, we must not overprotect children from their tests. It merely puts off the time when they will need to face their challenges. In a conversation with an extremely bright and "gifted" boy of thirteen, he spoke of how his parents' tardiness was driving him crazy. "And what do you do when they are late?" "I yell and scream at them to hurry up." "What virtue do you need in being honest and also respectful to them?" he was asked. "Oh." He smiled sheepishly and said, "I guess they are giving me a chance to develop patience."

Indulging or catering to children disempowers them. They grow up wanting there to be no problems or looking to others to solve them for them. They never develop their strength, and they go through life, as religious educator Tolbert McCarroll says, "holding tight to . . . mediocre images of

5

existence." There are many virtues that thrive only under conditions of challenge. How can one learn patience without having to wait? How would a child ever develop determination if life did not provide frustrations? How could we learn forgiveness without being hurt? If we don't use our virtues, we lose them, just like muscle tone in the physical body. Protecting children from their challenges is running interference with the Creator. As moral champions, our children deserve more respect.

Some of the best parents have children who make very bad choices or are born with a particularly difficult temperament. How you parent is your responsibility. How they turn out is a complex and mysterious process, with many influences other than yours.

The Opposititis Trap

We often unconsciously project onto our children the unmet needs we had as children. If something in our childhood caused us pain—usually a lack of love—we tend to go one of two ways. Either we unconsciously repeat our parents' behavior with our own children, or we go to the opposite extreme. A woman in a virtues workshop courageously admitted, "When I'm under stress, my mother comes out of my mouth."

We are far more aware of wanting to correct the sins of our parents when they emerge in our behavior than to catch the more insidious habit of opposititis. For example, if our parents were very judgmental and made their affection conditional on our performance, we want to give unconditional love to our children. What that may look like, unfortunately, is giving them carte blanche acceptance no matter what they do, whether they are being rude or courteous, kind or cruel. In doing so, we are ignoring their true needs for mastery and meaning. If our parents tended to be too affectionate and sloppily sentimental, we may hold our children at arm's length, giving them the respect and space we always craved. Meanwhile, they may be longing for more hugs.

The problem is that either way we are "reacting" to our own story rather than truly seeing our children. Our parenting becomes dictated by our needs and experiences rather than what is going on for our children. Rather than consciously treating our children as they need to be treated, we are treating them as we wish we had been treated by our parents. George Bernard Shaw said, "Don't do unto others as you would have them do unto you. They may have different tastes!"

The following true story illustrates a case of opposititis. Maria proudly invited her seven-year-old son, Robert, to show his school report card to Ellen, a visiting friend. Robert was immediately embarrassed and was reluctant to do so. As Maria went ahead and told Ellen about his grades, Robert became increasingly angry. "Mom, those grades weren't very good, ya know!" Maria replied with great tenderness in her voice, "But, sweetheart, it doesn't matter! All that matters is that you tried."

Robert shouted, "No!" at the top of his lungs and stormed out of the room. "I don't know what's got into him. Ellen, what do you think?" Ellen asked, "What gave you the idea to praise Robert for those mediocre grades? He's very bright and capable of much more." Maria explained that when she was in school, a little older than Robert, she had developed a learning problem and no one recognized it. She had suffered terribly from the shaming criticism heaped on her by her family and her teachers, who considered her a "stubborn underachiever." She was also labeled "lazy" at home and "dumb" by children at school. In giving Robert indiscriminate praise, Maria was simply giving him the opposite of what she had received.

Ellen gently suggested that perhaps Maria was giving Robert what she might have needed but not what he needed, which was encouragement to practice excellence, the challenge to do his best. "What if you ask him how he felt about his grades and then ask him what he wants for himself? What would excellence look like to him?"

When Maria hesitantly asked Robert what troubled him about showing his grades, he began to cry and said, "That wasn't my best, Mom. I could get A's if I wanted to." He and Maria had a talk about what he truly wanted for himself. Robert's face lit up when he was asked what goal he would like to set for himself to reflect his best. He became very excited about the mastery of excellence, which was in alignment with his purpose—to give life his best. The next term he was at the top of his class. When he graduated from high school years later, he had one of the highest grade-point averages on record and was honored in the local newspaper. (See Appendix A, Discussion Exercise 1, "Opposititis—'It Doesn't Matter.' ")

The "Chip off the Old Block" Syndrome

We also need to avoid trying to impose on our children the things we value about ourselves. We leave our legacy, and they leave theirs. Our values are helpful in giving them a place to stand, but they may well climb a higher mountain. Certainly they will climb a different one.

Seeing a child for who she is, a unique individual, calls for us to detach ourselves from any expectations we may have of what the basic nature or "virtues profile" a child of ours "should" have, especially in the service of our egos. If she seems to be a quiet child who likes to read and has only one or two friends, it is not our place to try to shape her personality into that of an outgoing socialite. If we happen to be shy and have some painful memories of social awkwardness, we may feel the need to push this gentle little soul in a direction that is not hers. In a virtues seminar for a television network, a successful puppeteer doing innovative production and design work for children's television shared during a virtues exercise that she had been labeled "shy" as a child. She wept as she expressed the awareness of how that label had deprived her of friends, had created a "script" of great loneliness. She was acknowledged for her trust and friendliness to reveal this in the group. It was fascinating that she had taken an area of difficulty in her life and found such a creative way to express her talents "behind the scenes."

Many people spend years feeling they are not enough no matter what they do. The disappointment of a parent is devastating to a child. When our children disappoint us—and they will—it is for one of several reasons. Some of these are:

- We may not be setting clear boundaries about the specific virtues we feel are called for in a situation.
- We have unreasonable expectations.
- We are failing to see the individual that our child is.
- We are reacting to some lack we feel in ourselves.
- They are having an off day—and need a little tolerance.

Of course, we have a desire to pass on what we have learned to our children, but the truth is that they meet life with a fresh perspective. It is far more empowering to focus on the virtue of excellence or purposefulness and then to discover, with great curiosity and openness, how your child will uniquely express these virtues in his life.

Isn't Love Enough?

You may be wondering, won't my children grow up all right if I just love them? It may seem unnatural to see ourselves in the role of spiritual caregiver, which requires us to hone and challenge and trust our children's ability to acquire virtues. Our instinct, from the time they are tiny and vulnerable, is to cuddle and protect them. This protective instinct is essential for their safety. To know that one is unconditionally loved and cared for is the foundation of all growth.

Play is the work of childhood. Children need lots of non-compulsory time, time for fun and silliness, cuddling and pure enjoyment. Their natural joyfulness requires it. Yet there are also moments of readiness for mastery and meaning to occur. At such times, a good mentor responds by encouraging children to find their edge, to practice the virtue to which the moment calls them, to give a situation their best effort—at gentleness, or generosity, or flexibility, or self-discipline. And there will be many times when we can only comfort and encourage, when we must watch our children face painful situations. Perhaps, in a sense, it is about knowing when to protect and when to step out of the way and let the Creator work with them. That is perhaps the greatest act of love a parent can offer.

The next chapter addresses the how-to's of spiritual parenting, the strategies for empowering children as champions.

⊰⊱ CHAPTER 2 ⊰⊱

What's a Parent to Do?

Parenting Principles and Practices in the Virtues Project

"Human happiness is founded on spiritual behavior." —ABDU'L-BAHA

Seeing a child as a separate, responsible, gifted individual full of potential virtues waiting to happen is the foundation of the parent-child relationship. The Virtues Project advocates a holistic approach to parenting which views the parent as:

- Educator
- Authority
- Counselor
- Guide

The five strategies of The Virtues Project are the how-to's of these roles and apply as much to one's own personal development as they do to being a parent. These strategies are being used in families, schools, prisons, social-service programs, faith communities and corporations around the world as ways of bringing out the best in ourselves and each other. The strategies are:

1. Speak the Language of the Virtues
2. Recognize Teachable Moments
3. Set Clear Boundaries
4. Honor the Spirit
5. Offer the Art of Spiritual Companioning

The roles of a parent are like facets of a diamond. In each role, parents can call on one of the strategies as their primary tool. The Language of the Virtues provides a tool to be applied in all the roles a parent plays as illustrated here:

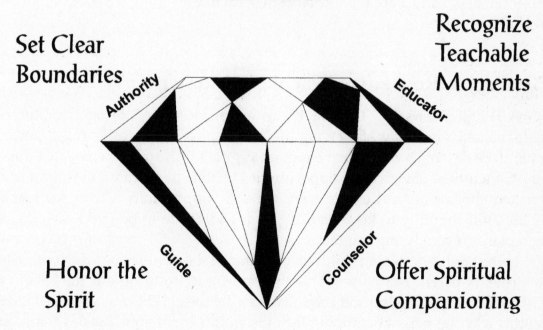

Always Speak the Language of the Virtues

Set Clear Boundaries

Authority

Recognize Teachable Moments

Educator

Honor the Spirit

Guide

Counselor

Offer Spiritual Companioning

Parent as Educator

To educate means "to bring forth" what already exists. The Virtues Project views a parent's first and most important role as that of a mentor to a child's inherent virtues. So a parent is a teacher, not a dictator, a guide and counselor, not a peer or pal. As an educator we are meant to support children to grow through life's many challenges and to help them turn the inevitable tests of life into victories.

The primary work of parenting is paying attention, and the quality of attention is directly proportionate to the degree of concentration. To pay attention to children is to be aware of what they are capable of today that they were not capable of yesterday, and to treat them with enormous respect as the purposeful beings they are. It is also to see your unique child as the individual she is. The healthy development of identity comes as parents and caregivers truly see the persons children are and skillfully bring out the best in them.

Strategies 1 and 2 are the tools most useful to the parent when acting in the role of educator.

Strategy 1. Recognize Teachable Moments

A Tlingit elder said, "Life is for learning our lessons." Recognizing teachable moments is a way of viewing life as an opportunity for learning, recognizing the day-to-day stuff that happens as grist for the mill of character. Tests and difficulties are viewed as opportunities to hone our virtues. In Chinese the written characters for the word *crisis* mean "opportunity." It is our teachability, our humility to keep learning, that allows life to be lived with joyful acceptance, even during tough times.

In the course of raising children, a teachable moment is one which calls for a virtue. A parent recognizes it as an opportunity to bring out the best in a child, or to acknowledge and reinforce a virtue the child is already practicing. In this way the parent is tapping into the child's innate qualities of character rather than just trying to manage behavior. Calling a child to a virtue—naming a virtue which is called for in a given situation—shows her that she is capable of practicing it. Ironically, when mastery and meaning are involved in the interaction, children are far more responsive than if a parent barks orders, shames them, or tries convincing arguments (which usually fail to convince!). There are many teachable moments each day for even the youngest child. You can say to a three-month-old waiting to be fed, "You're being really patient," or if they are starting to fuss, "Be patient, sweetheart. I will feed you as soon as I wash my hands."

From Shaming to Naming

It is time that the practice of shaming children is replaced by the practice of naming their virtues. How many adults suffer poor self-esteem that began with the sense of shame they experienced in their families of origin? They struggle all their lives because of deep feelings of unworthiness or inadequacy. Poor self-esteem develops from receiving little or no feedback, being repeatedly criticized, receiving physical or mental abuse, feeling invisible, or feeling unloved.

We have heard many painful stories and seen many tears in virtues workshops when we ask people to identify a name they were called, a label they received from their parents or those who raised them. They speak of labels such as stupid, lazy, shy, bad boy, fatty, pigheaded, slow as molasses, and a string of obscenities which have little meaning but sure enough got across a message of unworthiness or "not-enoughness."

Ehsan, a man raised in the Middle East, told of a turning point in his life, at the age of six, when his father had just finished building a bath, a large tiled room beneath their house. He was so excited, he ran down the steps, shouting, "Daddy! Daddy! I want to take a bath!" "You stupid boy," his father replied, "don't you know it will be hours before the water will fill the bath? Get away from here." What a teachable moment lost. What a desecration of this child's enthusiasm. How would it have been for Ehsan if instead his father had named his virtues instead of shaming and labeling him? For example, "I see how enthusiastic you are about the bath. It will take patience to wait for the bath to fill." They could have shared a moment of thankful appreciation together, watching the water fill the bath. Instead what happened is that Ehsan, red-faced with shame, ran up to his baby sister's room and climbed under her cradle to cry. The cradle became dislodged, the baby fell out and started screaming, and both parents came running. Ehsan ever after was called "Destroyer." A small moment in life which is still in the healing process for this man, now a father himself. (See Appendix A, Discussion Exercise 2, "From Shaming to Naming.")

Use Virtues, Not Labels

Labeling children or name calling is one of the surest ways to stick children with a negative self-image. Many of us label our children unintentionally when we are angry or disappointed. "Why are you being so stupid?" "Don't be an idiot." "What's wrong with you?" "Are you crazy? You could have blinded your sister throwing a sharp pen near her face." This is a form of shaming which sends a strong, disempowering message. It robs the child of moral choice. Children tend to believe their parents' words as absolute truth and identify with labels as if they are the truth. They will live down to labels if they hear them too often. A child who commits an impulsive act, and they all do, is in a teachable moment. "James, that was a dangerous thing to do. Your sister could have been hurt. How could you have used self-discipline to stop from throwing that pen?" Matter-of-factly naming the act and some virtue required in the situation gives the child a chance to reflect on the meaning of the moment and the virtue he needs to master. Having said that, there are times when it is perfectly appropriate to show anger, if it is in the form of clarity rather than adding violence to violence. The stronger the emotion, the greater the impact. Stating the unacceptability of an act and naming the missing virtue in a strong, command voice will not be forgotten, unless that is the only voice the child is used to hearing.

What is even more empowering is to catch the child later in the act of committing a virtue of self-discipline, or gentleness, or carefulness and acknowledging it. "I see you're being gentle with your sister."

Even labeling children positively can backfire and put too much pressure on them to perform. They grow up giving themselves away, living in the confines of a narrow, rigid role. A woman who was called "little mother" in appreciation for her helpfulness as the child of an overworked mother with ten children has found herself in the role of caretaker all her adult life. She married an alcoholic she has taken care of for years, and has great difficulty believing that she has the right to play, to enjoy non-compulsory time for just being, or to receive nurturing herself.

One of the most common ways we label children is the use of the vague

14

terms "good girl" and "bad girl." In a teachable moment, you are specific by using the language of virtues. "That was helpful" or "Please be considerate. Use your quiet voice." (See Appendix A, Discussion Exercise 3, "Recognize Teachable Moments.")

When we see children clearly, we know that they are like rich mines containing many gems of virtue. To bring out the best in them is to mine their gems.

Change Enabling to Empowering

Most parents are comfortable in the role of caregiver giving love, affection, and protection, and perhaps this part of parenting comes the most naturally. To be a caregiver who is also an educator means to be wary of the need we may have to overprotect by shying away from our child's spiritual challenges, by diluting or deflecting their spiritual lessons. The guiding principles for an educative parent are:

- Avoid doing for children what they can do for themselves
- Do for children what they cannot do for themselves

Allowing a child to take on a new responsibility, without expecting perfection but encouraging him in his early efforts, builds confidence and responsibility, two essential virtues in his moral fibre. Having him pour his milk, at first with your hand over his, then on his own and then acknowledging his responsibility, builds honest self-esteem. "You're being responsible, pouring your own milk" will be met with a proud nod.

It takes wisdom to know the difference between those times when we are to encourage our children to stretch and times they need our direct help. A tender scene we witnessed was when a father was speaking with his nine-year-old son about spending time with a friend who was encouraging him to steal. "Son, what happens when you are with Randy?" The boy sat very still and said, "I just feel tempted to take the candy. I just do what he says." "Honesty is really important, son. Would it help if I stopped you from seeing Randy for a while?" The boy began to cry tears of relief and said, "Yes, Dad, it would." Dad held him for a while, and then said, "I honor you for your honesty to come and tell me about this and to know what help you needed." This parent could have tried another tack, asking, "What would help you to be assertive with Randy so that you do what you want instead of listening to him?"

Although we want to support our children in daily teachable moments, we need to be aware of times when they are unable to handle a situation. Watch carefully for signs of readiness. If they are not prepared to handle a situation, we must handle it for or with them. We don't throw them to the wolves. Whether it involves monitoring TV programs or the movies they watch, other children whose influence they are not prepared to resist, or too much free time on their hands, we need to be aware of what is appropriate for our children to handle and what they are truly ready to handle. (See Appendix A, Discussion Exercise 4, "Ready or Not.")

Avoid the Abuse of Guilt

To help children develop the best within them is to continually address their higher self. Guilt is a gift. It is the "still, small voice" of conscience. It is the stop sign of the soul, a signal from the source of their virtues that something is not right. However, guilt does not tell a child what is right. Children need the language of the virtues to point them toward what they ought to be doing.

Guilt can be easily abused by parents who shame a child for making a mistake or doing something unacceptable. It is essential, as a respectful educator, that we guard a child's self-esteem by recognizing the tenderness and effectiveness of her burgeoning conscience.

In Virtues Project personal-development retreats, we speak of replacing "the internal critic" with "the gentle observer." It is far more inviting to view our mistakes with love and gentleness, vigilant to the virtues we intend to practice at the next teachable moment, rather than taking a self-indulgent bath in guilt. Guilt only serves us as a signal for change, not as a lifestyle!

What If Your Child Does Something Really Terrible?

Perhaps the most difficult time to stay within the educative model without sliding into shaming children is when they take us by surprise by doing something really terrible or unacceptable, such as stealing, destroying property, lying, intimidating or hurting another child in a cruel way. Almost all children do these things, no matter how much guidance or love they receive from us. But when they happen, our immediate natural response is to be shocked and ashamed. We wonder, "Where have I gone wrong bringing up this horrible child?"

The key to handling these situations effectively is to use the virtue of detachment to stop ourselves from being overly surprised and instead focusing on how to engage a child's conscience, sense of honor, justice, love, etc. Those virtues are in there, but sometimes it takes masterful mentorship to bring them to the fore. When a child does something really terrible, what is a parent to do? This is not the time to analyze why the child did it. "Were you angry at your sister when you picked up the rock?" That merely lets him off the hook. It is no time to explode in surprise. "How dare you?" "What's wrong with you?" "How could you?" Such vague expressions of horror do nothing to build conscience. We end up feeling guilty, and may be tempted to placate the child later. The following steps help to engage a child's conscience without shaming him or rescuing him, and without adding insult to injury.

- Stop the behavior.
  Take the rock out of the child's hand.
- Name a specific virtue.
  "Stop! This is dangerous! You are not being peaceful."
- Explain briefly how this is wrong.
  "It is never okay to use weapons when you are angry. People get hurt."
- Immediately give a consequence.
  "Go into the house right now and take a time-out."
- Encourage the child to make reparation.
  Afterward, invite the child to talk about what happened and to make reparation. "What happened?" After listening, ask, "How can you make up to your friend for forgetting to be peaceful?"

The healthy use of guilt allows the child to pay for the crime, explain his understanding of why he received a consequence and make reparation. Then it is essential to encourage him in future efforts to express anger peacefully.

The Family Virtues Guide is being used in many prisons around the world, restoring hope in adults who have done something really terrible. It is helping them to reclaim their virtues and reminding them that they are always more than the worst thing they have ever done. And that growth is never finished.

Be a Teacher, Not a Preacher: Don't Use the Virtues to Moralize

With all due respect to religious preachers who serve their faith, we are referring here to the habit parents have of giving lectures. The Virtues Project does not condone prissy morality. Teaching virtues as an educator is quite different from being a moralizer or lecturer. The virtues language, like any tool, can be misapplied and used as manipulation. That would be a sad mistake. Acknowledging children and reflecting to them your respect when they are showing an effort to practice a virtue, and calling them to a virtue when they are out of alignment with it, is very different from inappropriate preaching. Do you remember the lectures your parents gave you, or the daydreams you entertained to drown them out? The following examples of responses when a child is having trouble sharing may help to clarify the distinction between preaching and teaching.

Child pulls toy truck away from his playmate:

PREACHING PARENT: "You should share and be generous, Johnny. If you can't, you'll have to play alone." Even worse, "No one will like you."

TEACHING PARENT: "Johnny, be generous to your friend. Which toy would you like to share with her?" or "What would help you to share that toy peacefully?" or "Be generous, Johnny. Do you want to take turns with the truck or share some other toys?"

The word *should* is usually a good indicator that preaching is occurring. There is a shaming quality to it, and it usually results in a child reacting with tears or anger, whereas with firm but gentle teaching, children tend to calm down and see their options more clearly. This, of course, strengthens their ability to make moral choices, the choice to be just, to be generous, to choose caring over selfishness.

Recognizing teachable moments is closely linked to speaking the language of the virtues.

Strategy 2. Speak the Language of the Virtues

Language has great influence to empower or discourage. Self-esteem is built when shaming, blaming language is replaced by acknowledging each other for the virtues we see or calling each other to the virtues that are needed. If you fill a home, a school, or a workplace with words such as lazy, stupid, and bad, that is the behavior which follows, but if you use words such as courage, helpfulness, and flexibility, you are empowering those behaviors, whether in a child, an employee, or a friend.

Tap the Power of Language to Shape Culture

The language of the virtues can help change a family culture in a way that enhances strong family values. The virtues themselves provide a simple language of spirituality, of mastery and meaning, which parents may use to acknowledge effort and growth in their children. When children are acting on their lower impulses, parents can also use the language of virtues to call them back to the best of which they are capable in that moment. Rather than label a child as good or bad, a great kid or a problem child, the virtues themselves become the standard by which children can bring themselves to accountability, the standard against which they can assess their actions. For example, in a home where the virtues language is used, a child may think, "Today I had trouble with patience, but I was helpful when I set the table." The virtues could become the most common words used in family interactions.

Obviously, everyone in the family, from a toddler to a grandparent, can benefit from the gentle and honest scrutiny of the virtues. It is very empowering to decide together the core virtues which your family values most. You may decide to become a model of peace in the world by creating a "peace zone" in your home, finding ways to resolve conflict which are an expression of peacefulness. One family with young children has a "peace rug" which they pull out when consultation is needed to resolve angry feelings. You may decide that service is one of your core virtues and create a special savings account for gifts to needy people.

A family living in a city that becomes very cold in winter consulted together about what they would like to do to be of service. One frigid wintry day they set out to go around the city to observe people living on the street to find out what they needed. When they got home from this special tour, the father asked, "What did you notice?" The five-year-old said, "I saw them shiver and rub their cold hands." "What do you think they need?" "Mittens!" she shouted with excitement. The family went around collecting mittens from secondhand stores and then walked through the streets giving them out to homeless people.

Tap the Power of Language to Transform

Every one of a child's spiritual gifts, which are within them in potential, can be used or misused, remain dormant or become developed. For example, if a child has a natural tendency for high energy and wants more of everything—more time to play, more ice cream, more books to read—this can develop into enthusiasm, devotion, and purposefulness or, if mislabeled and criticized, can lead to greed, aggression, and selfishness. "You're so greedy" labels the child and gives her that as a life script, whereas calling her to a virtue brings her to awareness of what she can learn: "You need to practice some moderation with that chocolate" or "You are really enthusiastic about reading tonight, Susie. It will take some self-discipline just to have two stories instead of three, won't it?"

Every child is potentially the light of the world and its darkness. A child who has a strong personality can become a leader or a bully depending on how he sees himself mirrored in a parent's eyes. What determines the difference is how he is trained and educated, the images and models he is exposed to, and the parent's skill at challenging and directing his natural tendencies.

The extraordinary responses one sees from both children and adults, when naming their virtues, are linked to the fact that the virtues are the attributes of the soul, and we believe it is the soul which responds. A television interviewer once said, "How can you turn away when you are being called by your true names?"

Virtues are also the language of the soul. We know of countless examples of how powerfully people respond to having their virtues acknowledged, perhaps for the first time. A group of young offenders in a virtues-sharing circle in prison began to cry and open up when their virtues were acknowledged by each other, the facilitator, and the corrections officer who was standing guard. A twelve-year-old girl who had committed murder in order to join a gang at the age of ten, said, "I knew I would need a new lifestyle when I get out of here. Now I know what it's going to be. I'm going to live by the virtues. They're my gifts. They're me."

Use Virtues to Acknowledge

Self-esteem is the sum total of the accurate, positive things we know about ourselves. Children, and adults as well, need a good deal of mirroring when they are making an effort to develop a virtue. They need to be told what their behavior looks like, to have it noticed and acknowledged, not in terms of pleasing you but of honoring their own nature. Look for signs of effort and then reward them, not with candy but a virtues acknowledgment. You shouldn't be constantly acknowledging everything children do that pleases you—that would breed overdependence on praise. Rather, give virtues acknowledgments at those teachable moments when a child legitimately deserves to be acknowledged. This is what leads to inner strength and authentic self-esteem.

The most important time to acknowledge a virtue is when children are struggling with a virtue which doesn't come easily to them. The most meaningful teachable moments occur when you see a child making an effort to master an as yet undeveloped virtue. In past generations some strange notions existed that praising children would somehow "go to their head," causing them to "rest on their laurels." Both expressions seem a bit dim. When a person of any age is showing uncustomary courage or a tender move toward consideration, that is just the time to say, "I see your courage," or "That was considerate of you. Thank you." A fearful person showing courage or a typically self-centered person showing consideration is just the person who needs that little bit of emerging light to be mirrored back to them. In this way the language of virtues helps us to remember who we really are.

Do use moderation and wisdom. You don't want to overdo praise, even in the name of virtues. Children are quite sensitive to the justice and honesty of your responses to them. The human spirit has an uncanny ability to recognize the ring of truth. Children themselves know when they have done well, when they truly merit recognition. That may be why some children get very upset in the face of undeserved or excessive praise. Undeserved praise is almost as troubling to their spirits as criticism. When virtues are the focus of an acknowledgment, children receive the most effective mirroring possible. It allows them to see themselves.

Acknowledge effort by noticing, looking, smiling, or a gentle touch. It doesn't always have to be in words. It is the spirit more than the words that communicates. However, mirroring with the language of the virtues is useful when a child needs to be told what her behavior looks like. "I saw you being tolerant and forgiving with your friend today when she grabbed your truck" to a child prone to aggressive reactions mirrors to her the virtues you saw in her, thereby awakening and strengthening them. "I noticed you were quite assertive with your friend today when she grabbed your truck" when a child tends to let other children violate her boundaries awakens and strengthens her capacity to stand up for her rights.

There are a number of ways to give a virtues acknowledgment:

"I honor you for your courage to . . ." (name the specific situation or action)
"I want to acknowledge your courage to . . ."
"I see your courage."
"That took a lot of courage."
"It was courageous of you to . . ."
"You are being courageous."

You may also say, "Thank you for your consideration" (or helpfulness, or kindness) when the child has done something which directly affects you. Please do not overdo the use of "Thank you" such as "Thank you for being peaceful." The object is not to lessen the noise level for your comfort alone; it is for the child to learn the lesson of peacefulness. Overdoing thanks places you at the center of their conscience instead of their conscience at the center of themselves.

(See Appendix A, Discussion Exercise 5, "Virtues Acknowledgments.")

Use Virtues to Correct

Children "misbehave" for many reasons—because they are tired, because they have it in them to do destructive things, because they sense our tension, because they want to . . . and on and on. When a parent as educator puts a stop to negative behavior, he is being just as loving as when he applauds a child for effort. As a spiritual mentor the parent is ever alert to times when children are falling short of their best efforts at that moment. She is giving children security by not allowing them to go too far in hurting themselves or others.

When a child does something wrong or makes a mistake, the most empowering way to respond is to recognize the teachable moment involved. How many times have you experienced a vague look on a child's face when you say, "Stop that!" And they are not about to ask you what you mean. Calling the child to the virtue or virtues involved sets a context for the meaning of what they are doing. It reminds them of their spiritual work, and they often respond in a soulful way. There is an alertness to the call to virtue, an openness to hearing what you are saying.

Also, calling a child to a virtue tells them what you actually expect. It is very hard to stop doing something. It is much easier to focus on what to do than what not to do. "Stop hitting your brother" focuses on the child as a hitter. "Be peaceful. Use your voice" is far clearer as a message that you expect the behavior to change.

There are a number of ways to give virtues corrections:

"Please be kind."

"What would help you to be peaceful right now?"

"I need some consideration right now. Would you please turn down the music?"

"Be patient."

"This is going to take a lot of patience."

"How can I support you to be self-disciplined about remembering your homework?"

"What virtue do you need to call on right now?"

A three-year-old named Anita who had become quite adept at both responding to and speaking the language of the virtues herself was struggling to put her boots on, with her mother hovering and rushing her. Anita said, "Mom, do you think you need to call on a virtue right now?" "What virtue do you think I need, honey?" "Patience would probably help you right now," said the child tactfully. The next day, her mother wouldn't let Anita go into the yard just before dinner. "Mom, I think you need to call on a virtue!" she pouted. "Oh?" said Mom, not as receptive as the day before. "You need the virtue of

'Letness'!" "No, dear," said Mom, stifling a smile, "you need to call on the virtue of obedience." "Oh," she said, and a sheepish smile crept over her face.

Name the Act, Not the Actor

Whether it is a teachable moment in which you are naming something positive you see or calling a child to a virtue they are forgetting, it is essential to preserve self-esteem. The way to do this is to name the act and not the actor.

Examples of *inappropriate* virtues acknowledgments:

"You're so responsible."
"You're a kind person."
"You are always serving other people."
"You're Mommy's little helper."
"You're a good boy."

Examples of *appropriate* virtues acknowledgments:

"You're being so responsible to make your own bed."
"That was a kind thing to do."
"How gentle you are being with the baby."
"I respect the way you serve others."
"Thank you for being so helpful this morning. Making the lunches made a
    big difference in getting us all ready on time."
"I honor you for your courage to go to the bus by yourself."

Examples of *shaming* virtues corrections:

"You never play peacefully."
"Why can't you remember to be courteous?"
"I wish you had some self-discipline."

Examples of *empowering* virtues corrections:

"Please play peacefully now."
"What would help you to be peaceful with your anger?"

"You can be courteous. Please try harder."

"It takes a lot of self-discipline to do homework, doesn't it?"

"You may not be unkind to your sister."

"That was a kind thing to do" is a far kinder way to acknowledge a child than to say, "You are so kind," which labels him and gives him a queasy feeling about accepting unjust or exaggerated praise. "You forgot to be kind" is a kinder way to correct an unkind act than to label the child with a phrase such as "How could you be so mean?"

Make specific, positive requests. Addressing specific behavior with the virtues enables children to see themselves in process rather than stuck with some trait they sense pleases other people. The goal of virtues acknowledgments and corrections is to build character, to awaken and strengthen the child's innate virtues, not to reinforce people pleasing. Having said that, it is precisely the pleasure of the parent that is the major reinforcer for a child's behavior, so feel free to let your pleasure show as you respectfully acknowledge the qualities you see emerging in your child.

(See Appendix A, Discussion Exercise 6, "Virtues Corrections.")

Be Specific and Accurate

The most powerful virtues acknowledgment is one which is focused on a virtue which accurately reflects the core issue, the meaning of what the child is doing, or needs to be doing. "I honor you for your courage," when a child is attempting to do something scary, like going to school for the first time, is much more powerful than "I honor you for your caring," which isn't what the teachable moment is about in that case. In the face of fear, virtues such as courage or confidence or determination are what we need to lean on. Those are the spiritual lessons involved. By asking yourself, "What is the lesson here?" you will be able to identify the virtues relevant to a given teachable moment.

Any good teacher has the respect of her students, and there is a gentle, reliable order maintained in the classroom. Parents serving as the first educators also need to create an environment which is based on gentleness, respect, and order.

Parent as Authority

Strategy 3. Set Clear Boundaries

When it comes to authority, what's a parent to do in the face of so much conflicting advice? In North America there is more confusion about authority than perhaps any other issue of parenting. The relationship between parents and children has become confused, with parents feeling ambivalent about using authority and fearful of "doing it wrong" or damaging the child's psyche. Yet the lack of clear boundaries in a family creates a climate of constant arguing and power struggles, hardly supportive of anyone's peace of mind. Many parents, wanting to do it right, wonder how they can use authority without damaging a child's self-esteem. It is a legitimate question.

An Educative Model of Authority

There are four ways we typically relate to parental authority, each of which has great impact on the quality of life in our families:

1. Permissive, which in its extreme is a form of neglect
2. Dominant, which can be oppressive
3. Democratic, which invites conflict and power struggles
4. "Sliding," which is to shift back and forth between all three, leading to chaos

Permissive

Parents who tend to be laissez-faire and permissive avoid authority. It may be because they are confusing any use of authority with the Victorian, dictatorial model in which children were devalued. Often it is because they themselves felt devalued or experienced abuse at the hands of overly strict, dominant parents and they don't want to inflict that on their own children. Sometimes this model occurs simply because a parent is so overwhelmed trying to survive that there is little time or energy left for creating any sort of order at home. Sometimes permissiveness comes from downright confusion over what's right. Some say it would actually be better to risk doing it wrong in the name of clarity rather than to be chronically ambivalent, since confusion in a parent automatically creates anxiety in a child. One definition of a deprived child is one whose parents have no clear expectations.

A family with no clear parental authority is actually a leaderless group. A child without clear boundaries is like a person without a job description. Imagine yourself on a job in which your supervisor walks in the first day and says, "Do a good job," but fails to give you a job description. How is this different from parents who want their children to "be good," but give them no guidelines? There are no clear expectations, no goals. How would you ever know if you are doing well? How would you feel valued? Even more important, how would you be able to meet your needs for mastery and meaning in the work?

Dominant

At the other extreme, dominant parents are constantly in control mode, making for a constricted, unhappy, and often rebellious atmosphere at home. For dominant parents, guilt and shame are used to force children into compliance. This can be done without ever lifting a finger if the parent is a skilled, guilt-inducing manipulator. Such a home breeds children who are placaters, people pleasers, or rebels. In many cultures, caning or other kinds of physical force are the primary way that parents assert their authority. Unfortunately, this too often escalates to serious violence, causing deep, irremediable shame in a child and reinforcing their notion that they are "bad." It violates their sense of hope and destroys their sense of worth. It is not conducive to awakening their virtues. In dominant families, children tend to leave home as soon as they can.

Democratic

Many of today's parenting programs advocate a democratic or egalitarian approach to family life in which each family member is equally valued, parental authority is seen as inappropriate, and children's judgment is given equal weight. It sounds good, but it doesn't work. Everything is up for discussion. When parents and children have an equal voice, there is chaos and confusion and an invitation to argue constantly. The unity of the family is continually compromised, and there is certainly no lasting peace. Equality of value does not mean equivalence of function. To be equally valued does not mean that parent and child should have equivalent roles.

Because their need for order and predictability is so strong, if there is a vacuum of authority, children will fill it themselves and become the authority. There are many tyrannical children who unhappily rule the household with their moods, their resistance, and their anger. Often these children are out of control because their parents have misunderstood the authentic need for reasonable parental authority.

Sliding

The parent who slides back and forth between the permissive and the dominant is the most unhappy, and their children often tyrannize them. "I've tried everything," they often say, "these kids are just impossible." Trying everything is a primary symptom of sliding. Sometimes sliding occurs because of the guilt parents experience about the little time they have to spend with their children, especially in homes where both parents work outside the home, or a single parent is struggling to work, raise the children, care for the house, and so on. Economic and other pressures can lead to a stressed-out, overly burdensome lifestyle in which time seems stretched to the limit. Whether through guilt or confusion, the net effect is that many of us are so uncertain of our proper role that our children are often given too much power and not enough guidance. In this model the parent becomes a manipulator, trying to coax, cajole, or convince children, but children are magnificent learners and so they tend to outdo their parents at manipulation. When that happens, the parent feels put upon and slides into helpless anger, lashes out, then feels remorse and guilt, so begins to placate the child, and so the cycle continues, with no one winning—and no one learning to develop their virtues.

Sitting on the shore of a lake one hot summer day, we watched as a woman waded around after her belligerent six-year-old daughter, begging, cajoling, and pleading with her to wear a hat, giving her one reason after another. The child simply moved farther away, saying, "No. I don't have to. I'm not wearing it. I don't have to listen to what you say!" The mother was embarrassed, seemed to feel helpless, and finally stood there, hat in hand as the daughter splashed off. Then she took a deep breath, summoned her strength, waded quickly toward the girl, and caught her by the wrist. "You have to wear the hat," she yelled. The child began kicking and screaming, was bodily dragged out of the water, off the beach to the car, screaming her version of obscenities at her mother the entire time.

What was missing here? The mother slid from behaving in a permissive, helpless fashion, triggering a disrespectful response from her daughter, to a dictatorial mode, which triggered rage and further disrespect. The child did not wear the hat, and both mother and daughter lost the beauty of being at the lake. They also lost a precious teachable moment. Mother could have set clear boundaries before the child went into the water—"If you want to go in the water during this hot time of day, you will need to wear your hat." The message would have been clear. If the daughter had said, "I don't have to listen to you. I'm going in without my hat," the mother could have said, "Be respectful, Rebecca, and the boundary is, you can either go in the water with your hat on or stay under the tree with me." Most children in the face of a gentle, assertive approach would choose to obey.

The Educative Model

The Virtues Project is based on a model of parenting which is neither permissive nor dominant, nor does it advocate that parent and child have interchangeable roles and equal say. It is based on a model of the parent as educator. The authority of a parent is in the service of a child's learning. Authority is used to help the child develop virtues, the gifts within, just as a good coach uses discipline to help an athlete to develop all of his talents and strengths. Authority is not abused in service of a parent's need to dominate or to be pleased. If we are willing to accept the responsibility of leadership as service, we must sacrifice the wish for our children to love and approve and agree with us at all times. A good coach doesn't consult an athlete about whether she feels up to a regimen of running every morning at five o'clock. A good coach takes the responsibility to take that athlete to the edge. We have to give up being a pal who sometimes educates in order to be an educator who sometimes can be a pal. Our children will have lots of friends in their lifetime, but only we have the privilege of serving as their first mentors.

The goal of effective parental authority is to enable children to develop their own inner authority, a sense of personal responsibility, and an ability to make conscious moral choices. The younger children are, the more dependent they are on a fair and loving parent to guide and discipline their behavior. Clear, reasonable discipline gives children the foundation for self-discipline. Dictionaries define *discipline* as "training that develops self-control" or "training intended to produce a specified character or pattern of behavior." The patterns of behavior an educative parent focuses on are the virtues.

Give Children R&R: Routines and Rituals

Children crave clear boundaries. Their natural need for mastery and meaning requires a sense of order. They want to know where the track is and where the finish line is and what it means to be a good athlete, a good son or daughter. Without boundaries the world is simply too overwhelming. In their early years, they also crave predictability. The establishment of routines, rituals, and rules gives them a sense that all is right with the world. For example, young children love to have the same bedtime routine. Sometimes they want the same stories or the same prayers over and over.

When our younger son was three, he had an experience at a summer family retreat which turned him temporarily into a "tough guy." The cook was taking a break and began talking and laughing with him as we sat in rocking chairs on the porch of the lodge chatting with other parents. Suddenly he ran over to one of the posts and began to lick it, looking very proud of himself. The cook laughed uproariously. When we went over to investigate, the cook said, "I was just telling him what a tough little guy he is. I said, 'I bet you could lick this post.'" This seemed harmless enough until the next day when the camp nursery counselor said, "Your son keeps butting his head into other children. He just won't stop." That evening he scampered ahead of me down the long stairway to the lobby of the lodge. As I reached the landing, I looked down and saw a frail, elderly woman walking through the front door. I watched in horror as my son lowered his head and prepared to charge. I raced down the stairs and caught him just as he was about to make contact. This woman was the guest speaker, who had just traveled from Japan. In her eighties, she was considered an international treasure, and my son could have seriously hurt her. I knew I had to get through to him. Not yet aware of the language of the virtues, I was at a loss. Scolding didn't seem to get through to him, for he had latched on to toughness as his meaning and butting people as his mastery of choice! That night it came to me to make up a story about a goat, a kid who was so tough that none of the other kids wanted to play with him. His name, of course, was the same as my son's. In the story the kid wanders into the barn rejected and sad. An old billy goat counsels him that if he wants friends, he has to save butting for things like fence posts or trees, but not other goats. In the end he is welcomed back to the circle of his friends. My son responded immediately to this story of a character by his own name. The story became his ritual. He asked for it almost every night for the next several months. How I wish I had known also to call him by his true names—gentleness and peacefulness.

Older children and teens thrive on routines as well, for example, a regular time and day of the week to sit down and assign the weekly housework. It can be an enjoyable time, with a ritual such as pizza for dinner that evening, followed by a night just for the family to do something enjoyable together.

Ten Guidelines for Establishing Family Ground Rules

Establishing family ground rules is one of the best ways to set clear boundaries. To be effective, chosen boundaries need to be those to which everyone in the household is committed. They need to be simple, clear, measurable, and observable. They should reflect the vision or mission of the family, the purposes which guide what you are about as a family, not just something to rein in children's behavior. One simple way to establish this vision is to look at the list of virtues in this book, or add to the list if there are other virtues which have meaning for you, and choose a few core virtues which characterize the kind of family you want to be. For example, you may choose Peacefulness, Cleanliness, Respect, Consideration, and Responsibility.

Establishing family ground rules is perhaps the most important way to keep children feeling safe, both physically and emotionally. It also establishes limits which support mutual respect, peace, and justice in the family. The clearer children are about what is expected, the better their chances of feeling loved and accepted in their efforts to "do the right thing." Of course, they will test the limits to see how far they can go, not just to be contrary but in their natural quest for a zone of trust. "Where do the limits really exist?"

Every family has rules, whether spoken or unspoken—do's and don'ts. In an unhealthy family with poorly defined boundaries, children watch their parents like hawks to find out what is acceptable and what isn't on a given day. It makes them great manipulators but poor at setting personal boundaries in future relationships. A healthy family sets clear boundaries which can make things work smoothly, keep the children safe, and help everyone to respect each other's needs for privacy, space, consideration, and a fair distribution of the work of the household. Families with boundaries that are too tight, that honor obedience but not freedom, are oppressive. Families with boundaries that are too loose, which value freedom but not obedience, are chaotic. Authority in the service of learning balances obedience and freedom, and helps everyone in the family to grow. The family ground rules are a wonderful source of order and unity. They also raise the level of good feelings in the household because children know what is expected of them. The virtues are about "what being good looks like." A child's conscious choice to obey the family ground rules is one of her first spiritual acts.

Here are ten guidelines for setting effective family ground rules:

1. Be moderate.

There should be no more than five or six ground rules at any one time. There are many expectations you have, such as brushing teeth regularly and wearing clothes before leaving the house. You wouldn't necessarily need a ground rule to cover such things. What is the area of "teachability" which matters most at this time? As you create the ground rules, focus on the core virtues you feel most need to be practiced. Remember, they apply to everyone. Children watch what you do more than what you say.

2. Be specific.

Create ground rules which meet the specific needs of your family. Your way of practicing cleanliness, for example, should be relevant to the area in which you live. A family who lives in a muddy or snowy area may have a ground rule that shoes must always be taken off at the door. Many cultures around the world practice that as a form of courtesy. If your family moves to a place near a beach, you may want to initiate a ground rule of hosing off before entering the house.

3. Be positive. Base ground rules on the virtues.

Avoid expressing rules in the negative. This only draws attention and focuses awareness on negative behaviors. For example, you would not have rules such as:

1. No hitting
2. No eating in the living room
3. No swearing
4. No loud music
5. No going out before chores are done

Instead, word the rules positively and focus awareness on the virtues you feel the children or the family need to develop at this time.

OUR FAMILY GROUND RULES

Peacefulness. Our home is a peace zone. We work out conflict by listening with compassion and talking with honesty. We use our voices, not our hands, and we never use weapons.

Cleanliness. We keep our house clean by eating only in the kitchen and the family room. We put our things away (including toys) when we are finished using them.

Respect. We use respectful language to each other. We respect each other's privacy when a door is shut.

Consideration. We are considerate of others when we play music. We use quiet voices inside.

Responsibility. We share responsibility by doing our own chores on time.

4. Establish specific, relevant consequences (let the punishment fit the crime).

At the same time as the ground rules are made, you need to establish creative consequences for the possibility that a ground rule may be broken. The consequence should be set up in advance so that it is not dictated by your irritation level. You don't need to post these, but they do need to be explained when the ground rules are communicated.

Irrelevant example:

"If you hit another child, you will be grounded for a week."

Relevant example:

"If you forget to be peaceful and hit another child, you must stop playing and take a time-out."

Irrelevant example:

"If you go in the street, you will get a spanking."

Relevant example:

"If you are trustworthy, you can play in the yard. If you leave the yard, you will lose your right to play in the yard for the next half hour."

5. Use consequences which are educative, not punitive, restorative, not retributive.

The purpose of virtues-based discipline is to call children to the virtues. It is a form of restorative justice as opposed to retributive justice. In retributive justice the questions are "What was the crime?" "Who did it?" and "How should they be punished?" In restorative justice the questions are "What happened?" "Who was hurt?" (including the perpetrator), and "What do they need?" Consequences are not meant to make children feel bad about themselves but rather to restore them to the missing virtue, which often is justice. Give a child who has hurt someone the opportunity to make reparation. Invite him to come up with a way to make up to whoever has been hurt or disturbed by his behavior. This must be done respectfully, not a forced apology but a brief, creative brain-storming of what he feels would make up for what he has done. For example, a child who has been aggressive may think of something kind to do for the person who was hurt.

Justice also needs to characterize the consequences they receive for violating a ground rule. For example, the time length of a consequence should vary according to the age of the child. An effective length for time-outs is one minute for every year of the child's age. However, you can apply the same principle of justice if a teenager comes in two hours late, for example, that she then must come in two hours earlier the next Saturday night, or if a nine-year-old is ten minutes late for dinner, for example, he must be home the next night ten minutes earlier to help him remember to be trustworthy.

6. Be consistent.

Assume that children will test the limits, sometimes forget the rules or just be having a bad day. Regardless of the reason for the lapse, trustworthiness demands that the consequence be enforced automatically, not at your whim. This is not a time for mercy but for justice, so that children will learn that you say what you mean and you mean what you say—and that the rules are real.

When they know the rules are trustworthy, they begin to develop their inner authority, a sense that rules matter and keep them safe.

An eight-year-old boy named Tom was given a ground rule that when he comes home from school, after sitting all day, he is to go outside to play and not watch TV. The mother of another child called Tom's mother one evening to say how impressed she was that Tom had come over after school, and when her own son had turned on the TV, Tom had said, "I'll be outside when you want to play. Our family ground rule is we can watch TV after dinner." (See Appendix A, Discussion Exercise 7, "The Power of Consistency.")

7. Communicate rules clearly.

Write them out and post them on the refrigerator or somewhere at the children's eye level. The use of humorous illustrations will help reinforce the rules, especially for very young children and also for teenagers. Discuss the rules with your children. Be sure they understand the consequences for breaking any of the ground rules. Engage the children in creating a Ground Rules Chart. Their illustrations may well be more compelling than yours.

8. When children receive consequences, make sure they understand the reasons.

As soon as a consequence has been paid, call the child to account. "What was the consequence for?" and "Are you ready to play peacefully now?" With warmth and trust encourage them to keep trying. If the child is still angry or hurt, this is not a time for a lecture on why they shouldn't have done what they did. It is a time to listen to their feelings.

When we consult in schools around the world about creating "Virtuous Reality" in the classroom, we recommend that they replace the "naughty chair," still used in many countries, with the "courtesy corner," which reflects the principle that a child is always invited back to her best behavior rather than left feeling shamed. "Are you ready to be courteous now?" is the first thing children need to hear when their time-out is completed.

9. Make the ground rules nonnegotiable.

As parents who are the leaders of the family, you have the right and responsibility to decide which issues are negotiable and which are not. When you make a ground rule, make sure you can live with it and that it is truly nonnegotiable. Ground rules that are up for discussion or change are not true boundaries.

The time for discussion is before the ground rules are established. You may particularly want to consult mature children to receive their input into what the rules need to be and what would constitute fair ground rules that will serve as agreements to which they can wholeheartedly commit.

Children have a highly developed sense of justice, and if consulted about what the consequences should be for violation of a ground rule, they will often come up with more rigorous ones than you would have. Then you must stick to these consequences to create a high level of trust in your family.

10. Be flexible. Revise the rules over time.

From time to time, as children grow older, and as circumstances change for your family, such as a move to a new place, when a child begins school, an older child begins to drive, or a parent who has been working at home takes a job outside the home, you will need to create new ground rules which replace the old ones. This is an excellent time to engage the whole family in consulting about what ground rules will help sustain unity, create justice in sharing responsibilities, and keep everyone safe.

There are a number of ways other than the establishment of family ground rules to apply the strategy of setting clear boundaries. (See Appendix A, Discussion Exercise 8, "What Difference Can a Ground Rule Make?")

Give Choices Within Boundaries

One of the times we need to set clear boundaries beyond the ground rules we have for our families is when children (or adults) have choices to make. When children are small, most of their choices need to be given within predetermined boundaries. For example, they cannot choose where they are going to play since this is a safety issue. If given free choice, they could wander off, get lost, or expose themselves to danger. They must be given choices within boundaries, such as "Would you like to play in the backyard or the front yard?" or "Would you like to sit in your high chair and play while I'm cooking or in the playpen in the living room?" It is merely foolish to ask a two-year-old what he wants for breakfast. "Hmmm. Lessee. How about jelly beans and lemonade?" But it is very helpful to his budding discernment to offer him a choice within limits: "Today, would you like porridge or eggs for breakfast?" It is mere foolishness to ask a child, "Would you like to go to bed now?" At bedtime you might say, "It's bedtime. Would you like the story we read last night or a new one?"

When we fail to give choices within boundaries, we are begging for a power struggle, one our child is far more likely to win than we are. Kids just seem to have more perseverence. Also they use an entirely unique, deductive system of logic. "I want it, therefore there must be a way for me to get it." Worst of all is the "Just because" stance children can take when asked to justify their behavior. Best not to even try. Boundaries, on the other hand, have the power to move them, literally.

Chuckie was a memorable child we met at a small dinner party in the home of his parents. He was seated in one of the dining room chairs, his small four-year-old frame braced, with his hands clinging to the arms of the chair. The dialogue began:

MOTHER: (*in a sweet, lilting voice*) Chuckie, our dinner guests are here. Wouldn't you like to move out of that big chair into your high chair? (*A good start, but she lost it.*)

CHUCKIE: Nope.

MOTHER: (*in a more pleading tone*) If you don't, our guests will have nowhere to sit.

CHUCKIE: Uh-uh.

MOTHER: (*sweeter than ever*) Chuckie, won't you be more comfy in your own chair so you can see everyone?

Chuckie is unmoved.

When a parent gives a child too much power or leeway in decision making without setting parameters for their choices, the child almost always "wins" the battle of wills. However, it is in reality a loss, a loss of security. Children such as Chuckie who are given too much power have nightmares, wet the bed, and show anxiety in other ways. To be given power over their powerful parents is in a very real way a loss of security and trust. If Chuckie could articulate his feelings and thoughts, he might think, "If I have all this power over this grown-up who is supposed to be taking care of me, is anybody around here strong enough to protect me?"

Here's how the dining room scenario could have gone if Chuckie's mother had set clear, virtues-based boundaries and offered him choices within them:

MOTHER: Chuckie, it's time to move into your own chair now. The guests are here.
CHUCKIE: Nope.
MOTHER: (*picking him up and putting him in his high chair*) You can be courteous, can't you? Wouldn't Mrs. P. look silly sitting in your high chair?

Chuckie would probably get a chuckle out of this, but would also know that Mother meant business. Should he continue to rebel, or accelerate the struggle, Mother would again refer to the boundary and give him choices within it.

CHUCKIE: No, I don't wanna. I wanna sit in a big chair.
MOTHER: Chuck, you have a choice now. You can be obedient and courteous and join us for dinner, or have dinner in your room.

A creative and more flexible alternative is that you may wish to allow him to sit in a "big chair." You can do that if there are plenty of chairs, but don't do it if you have already insisted he sit in his high chair. If you chose this alternative, you would again call Chuckie to courtesy. "You may sit in a big chair tonight if you will be courteous to Mrs. P. and help your father get a chair for her."

(See Appendix A, Discussion Exercise 9, "Give Choices Within Boundaries.")

Set Boundaries When Virtues Are Violated

Setting a clear boundary is called for when justice or respect or some other virtue is being violated in your relationship with someone in the family, whether adult or child. If someone tends to be sarcastic or abusive in the way he speaks, you can decide what you are going to do. "If you speak respectfully, I will listen" or "I am willing to listen to you only if you speak respectfully," and walk away. Come back later and say, "Do you want to talk now?" If you are playing a game and the children start to rough-house, and you are not in the mood, you can say, "I will play as long as you are being peaceful," period. If the rough-housing begins again, just get up and do

38

something else. If they plead with you to come back, say as little as possible. "Maybe I will play with you tomorrow." This is not about power struggles or manipulation. Set your boundary and let your behavior speak for itself. Actions always speak louder than words, since ninety percent of what children learn comes from observation.

Set Boundaries to Prepare Children for New Situations

Another opportunity to set a clear boundary is when a new situation comes up. Give some thought to boundaries that will help things go smoothly. If you are taking a child to a meeting where she must remain quiet, tell her beforehand that she will need lots of self-discipline to sit quietly. Ask her what would help her to do that. She may think of the idea of bringing a pad of paper on which to draw quietly. Tell her ahead of time what the consequence will be if she is unable to stay within the boundary. Remember, this is not a punitive thing. It may be as simple as "The boundary is, there must be silence for the whole meeting. We have to be courteous to the people. Let's see how long you can use your self-discipline. If you feel you can't sit quietly any longer, whisper to me and we will go out to the lobby for a while."

A mother recently related a lovely story of how boundaries empowered her three-year-old daughter so that she could attend her grandfather's funeral. Jennifer's mother felt it important for her to have the opportunity to say good-bye to her grandfather, yet was concerned because Jennifer was an extremely active child with a very short attention span. She talked with her beforehand. "Jenn, it is going to take lots and lots of patience for you to sit quietly at Grandpa's funeral, but it is very, very important because people need to feel their reverence. Do you think you can do it?" "Yes, Mama. I want to come. I'll be really, really patient." On the day of the funeral, the mother said, "Jenn, I trust you to be really, really patient. And when you feel you can't be patient any longer, just squeeze my hand and we will walk out together." Jennifer's mother was amazed when the child sat through the entire funeral, still and quiet and more patient than she had ever been in her life. Jennifer's eyes shone when she went up to her grandfather's casket. Holding her mother's hand, she whispered, "Up," and her mother lifted her. She placed a rose on her grandfather's heart. What a spiritual triumph, especially for a child diagnosed with attention-deficit hyperactivity disorder!

(See Appendix A, Discussion Exercise 9, "Give Choices Within Boundaries.")

Four Principles of Discipline

The following simple principles can guide you as you create your family ground rules and practice setting clear boundaries instead of feeding conflict.

1. Link freedom to responsibility.

The greater the responsibility shown by children, the more freedom they are ready to handle. The more trustworthy children are, the more trust parents can give them. You could say to a sixteen-year-old who has faithfully kept the ground rule of a midnight curfew on weekends, "Josh, you have been very responsible about curfew and trustworthy about bringing the car back when you said you would. How would you like to take that camping trip with your friends you've been asking about?"

2. When it comes to safety, require simple obedience.

The beauty of ground rules is that they can eliminate parental yelling. When a child hears you yell, it should be an indication of danger. If a child is headed into the path of an oncoming car, it is essential that he respond to a parental command to stop. If direct commands are reserved for important times, they retain the power to influence. If a parent yells at a child continually, the most dangerous aspect of this is that the child may not listen when it really matters. Children become immune to power when it is overused and misapplied. A command from a passive, permissive parent will have the same effect. It is likely to be ignored. Children are very tuned in to their parents. They instinctively respond to changes in the parent's tone of voice. However, they can begin to "numb out" when there is too much or too little control.

3. Prevent power struggles.

It serves no one to live in a household where there is constant bickering. Avoid making a major issue over everything. Avoid preaching, nagging, and reminding. Let the ground rules stand and the consequences apply. When an order is called for, give it once, then ask the child to repeat it to be sure she understands it. Briefly name the virtue involved. If she later disobeys it, enforce the consequence and let it speak for you. Then call her back to the virtue involved.

(See Appendix A, Discussion Exercise 10, "What's Wrong with This Picture?")

Having family ground rules is an excellent way to prevent power struggles. The rule is clear. Children choose to obey it or not and receive a predetermined consequence if they choose to disobey. They should be acknowledged for the virtue of faithfulness or obedience or responsibility when they are obedient. Whether or not children have made a deliberate choice, having a consistent, automatic consequence teaches them cause and effect and personal responsibility for their choices. There need not be a battle of wills every time they "forget" to do a chore. There is no scene of pleading, preaching, or nagging. There is only the consequence. For example, if a child consistently neglects a chore, the chore can be doubled or a particular freedom can be dependent on his showing responsibility by having done the chore.

4. Always acknowledge effort and improvement.

One of the keys to successfully encouraging character development is to give positive feedback about improvement. It doesn't need to be gushy or excessive. It does need to be real. When any one of us makes an effort, which always involves some risk, that is when we need the most encouragement.

Since all that a child can become depends on education, opportunity, and effort, the most effective way to educate a child is to acknowledge and applaud her when you see effort. Their will is one of their greatest tools for spiritual growth. Whenever you see it being exercised, particularly when it takes rigorous self-discipline or patience to practice a developing virtue, that is the time for applauding children and cheering them on.

When you give your child a virtues acknowledgment such as "I notice you have been really peaceful with your brother lately. Good self-discipline" in a respectful and appreciative tone of voice, giving him a hug or a pat as you do so, it will help him to maintain his efforts. When acknowledgment is connected to a family ground rule, it is one of the clearest messages you can give to a child about what being "good" looks like.

Parent as Guide

Strategy 4. Honor the Spirit

Share Your Skills

Parents guide children in many ways. One is by sharing their knowledge, wisdom, and skills. Allowing children to participate in meaningful activity, gently guiding them to master their own skills, takes time. Allowing a child to stand on a chair and cook with you, or giving a child a simple job to do in your workshop, is a precious and valuable use of parental time. The language of the virtues can be woven through these experiences. "Mary, you showed a lot of determination today. You never used a wrench before, but when I showed you how, you kept trying until you got it." In giving children the freedom to explore their talents and abilities, you are honoring their spirit—their creativity, purposefulness, and excellence.

Share Your Family Stories

The sharing of stories about your family and yourself awakens a child's sense of meaning. Knowing the virtues that are special about this family—Grandfather's courage or Great-grandmother's humor—brings the spirit of family honor to life. It is very important that from their earliest years, you also listen to and draw out your children's own stories. Listening to their sleeping and waking dreams, just hearing them respectfully, honors children's growing spiritual awareness. It honors them as people of value. Dinner together is a wonderful time to invite each person to share the story of his day. Asking which virtue was involved enhances the teachable moments involved. (See Appendix A, Discussion Exercise 11, "A Family Values History.")

Create Routines of Reverence

The virtues offer a frame of reference, a context for a life lived purposefully and reverently. The Virtues Project approach helps children and adults to access meaning by awakening and touching their sense of the sacred. In our families we need routines of reverence, times for silence, reflection, or prayer.

Setting boundaries around your own need for reflection time models for children their right to do the same.

Having a special time for the family to experience reverence together is also very powerful. A sharing circle is one way to experience reverence as a family. Read a passage or a quotation from one of the holy books sited in the virtues section or read something brief from an inspirational source, followed by five to ten minutes of silent, closed-eyes meditation. Then allow each person to share, without cross talk or interruption, how that reading and the meditation spoke to them. When each person finishes sharing, the other family members acknowledge the person for a virtue they noticed. Then the next person shares.

One family has a special cloth they have embroidered with each person's name around the edges. When they meet as a sacred gathering, they place this special cloth on the floor and sit around it beside their own name. Each person places on their section of the cloth an object which has meaning for them. It could be a book they have been reading, a special toy, something they have found outside. They share one by one, and the rest of the family members acknowledge the one who has shared with the virtues they see.

One of the practices of The Virtues Project is called a "Virtues Pick." In this exercise, people either use *The Family Virtues Guide* by opening at random to a virtue or a set of Virtues Reminders cards with brief descriptions of the virtues. After blind-picking a virtue, each person reads or has the virtue read for them, shares with the group what is happening or how they feel that day, and then how the virtue speaks to them at this time, what gift is in it for them. After the sharing, during which the group has been silently present to the individual, they give virtues acknowledgments to the person.

Mark Special Times with Special Rituals

Children are natural mystics. They value ceremony and personal ritual as much or more than adults do. We all need to celebrate the mysterious and the special. When a young woman first menstruates, in some cultures she is given a special dress worn by her ancestors, or a special piece of jewelry. Taking your daughter out for dinner and giving her a necklace you have been keeping for this occasion tells her that it is meaningful and special that she has become a woman. Taking a young man or woman in their mid-teens to a place of natural beauty and sending them out to spend a night alone reflecting on their purpose and vision marks the life transition from childhood to adulthood as special. Having a ceremony and presenting a child who is going off to school for the first time with a special outfit or writing instrument says, "This is important and you are important."

These simple ways of supporting the sacred, of honoring the spirit, are not meant to serve as a substitute for formal worship. However, families of many faiths and cultures who do practice a particular religion find that these intimate practices enhance and personalize the faith experience.

What About God?

If it is important to you that your child develop a relationship with a higher power, start early in the child's life, when their sense of wonder and reverence develops most naturally. The words you use about that higher power, whether God or Creator or the Founder of your faith, need to be mentioned day to day. Whether you have specific religious beliefs or you see yourself as a "general practitioner" with an unstructured belief but strong spiritual values, the spiritual power in which you believe needs to be referred to in natural daily ways.

For a child, the mention of God as a powerful, loving Creator needs to be a part of normal life, not something reserved for worship services. Children may not be able to conceive of God in a broad, abstract way, but just as they can make a place in their lives for a relative or grandparent they have never seen, they can make a place for God. By the age of two, children know who all the VIPs are in their world. If God is to be one of them, start talking about God when your child is young.

A little boy, when asked to draw whatever he liked, began drawing away. When the teacher asked him what he was drawing, he said, "It's a picture of God." "No one knows what God looks like," said his teacher. "They will when I get through," he said.

Children pick up whatever attitude you have about this Being or Power, whether it is reverence, a sense of trust, or thankfulness for the gifts of life. They will find it perfectly natural for you to say things like "Let's thank the Creator for this beautiful day" or "God loved you so much that God created you and brought you into the world" or "If you need help, you can pray and God will hear you."

44

The virtues section of this book contains a very simple approach to God, woven into the various virtues. God is described as:

- Loving
- Wanting the best for us and from us
- One we can trust
- One who has the power to take care of us and our problems

The more central you wish the relationship with a Creator to be, the more you will engage your children in spiritual practices such as:

- Daily prayer
- Meditation
- Attendance at worship services
- Reverence for Nature

The child's natural sense of wonder is an enormous part of her spiritual experience in the early years. Looking at the natural world through the eyes of a small child is a wonderful way to develop your own reverence. My granddaughter May, at age three, after spending the afternoon in a park with her father, gazing at clouds, studying grass, running and laughing, said, "This was the most wonderful day of my life."

Another way to honor the spirit of our children is to serve as their spiritual companion. Many people treat children as if they are adults in training, incomplete human beings, yet they are miraculously complete and whole. Being a spiritual companion is to meet them in their wholeness and in their truth. The fifth strategy is about simple ways to companion children. (See Appendix A, Discussion Exercise 12, "A Confidence History.")

Parent as Counselor

Strategy 5. Offer the Art of Spiritual Companioning™

Counseling is a big part of a parent's job description. It seems as if every day with a child brings a skinned knee or a hurt feeling. To be a spiritual counselor is to offer more than your compassion. It is to support your child when he faces a moral dilemma. It is to assist the child to find resolution rather than doing his spiritual work for him. The virtues-based approach to the role of counselor is one which is highly respectful, and honors the child's ability to find his own truth in a context of virtues.

There is a big difference between sympathy, empathy, and companioning. Sympathy is when you feel sorry for someone, empathy is when you can feel their feelings, and companioning is when you bring compassion and detachment together so that you can walk intimately with others without taking on their feelings as your responsibility. The ability to witness another's feelings without needing to fix them is a powerful gift to give to anyone, but particularly to our intimates. Douglas Steen says, "To 'listen' another's soul into a condition of disclosure and discovery may be almost the greatest service that any human being ever performs for another."

What About Feelings?

The simplest way to serve as a child's spiritual companion is to be present to the child, especially when strong feelings come. Whether a child is feeling sad, mad, glad, or scared, it always helps to have a parent there as a respectful, loving, genuinely present witness. This is not a time to bring in one's own feelings or to take on the child's. Just meet the child. If she skins a knee and gets right up, you don't need to ask, "Did you hurt your knee?" If she takes a deep breath and lets out a scream, gather your detachment and compassion to hold her, to hear her, to comfort her. True comfort comes with simple acknowledgments such as "Ooh, that really hurt," "That was a nasty fall," or "Your knee really got banged," not deflections or rescues such as "We'll put some ice on it and then it will be all better," or minimizing: "Don't cry. It's just a little scrape." Don't encourage children to skip their feelings. Get the ice, but as you are doing so, you can honor the truth of their experience.

Serving as an educator and authority in a child's life in no way removes the need to be receptive and respectful of children's feelings. The Virtues Project does not condone the suppression of feelings in the name of virtue. The long-standing custom that children are to be seen and not heard must be replaced with the understanding that every person, especially a child, has the right to be seen, to be heard, and to be taken seriously. Listening to a child's feelings validates their experience and is essential to self-esteem. It is a powerful way for parents to model compassion, courtesy, and respect.

If a child experiences this respect from his parents, he will be free as an adult to honestly admit his own feelings, to accept those feelings with compassion, and then to use detachment to choose how he is going to act in light of his feelings. Your detached, compassionate listening lays the foundation for your child's emotional and spiritual health.

There are situations when it is not timely to draw out a child's feelings, namely when she has just acted in an aggressive manner. The appropriate response from the parent at such a time is to stop the behavior and give a consequence. After a consequence is given is often a time when feelings need to be heard. For example, after a time-out for an aggressive act has been completed, you may want to invite the child to talk about her anger. This is a dialogue in a home which has a boundary about the expression of anger through words rather than violence:

PARENT: What was the consequence for?
CHILD: 'Cuz I hit Robby.
PARENT: Are you ready to play peacefully now?
CHILD: Yes.
PARENT: Do you want to talk about what happened?
CHILD: I was just tired.
PARENT: What were you tired of?
CHILD: Robby really made me mad.
PARENT: How?
CHILD: He grabbed my stuff. He always does.
PARENT: He grabs it. Pretty annoying. Disrespectful.
CHILD: (*taking a deep breath*) Yes, it was.
PARENT: So, honey, when Robby grabs things and you're feeling mad, how can you be assertive with him? How could you show you're mad and be peaceful at the same time?
CHILD: I could tell him, if he does that again, he has to go home, right, Mom?
PARENT: That sounds like a good boundary. Very assertive.
CHILD: Okay, Mom, I'm gonna play now. 'Bye.

This is no time to preach. Preaching is unnecessary and annoying to a child who has already paid his "debt to society" through the consequence. Asking him what he has learned is a far more effective way to recognize a teachable moment. Taking the next step of listening to feelings when the child wants to and you have the time and energy to do it can be very empowering. When a parent then asks questions which help a child reflect on what virtue they could have used, it empowers the child's budding moral sense.

Help Children to Make Moral Choices

One of the most important spiritual activities for a child is her emerging capacity to make moral choices. Spiritual Companioning is an art and a skill with which to support children to discover their wisdom and discernment. It is quite a contrast to the typical approach taken by most loving parents when a child has a problem to be solved. What would any nurturing parent worth her salt do when a child is troubled or in conflict? She might listen for a while and then, of course, give the child the benefit of her wisdom. This actually deprives the child of his own wisdom—and the opportunity to seize a highly teachable moment, the opportunity to resolve a moral dilemma.

It is far more empowering to enter into a child's feelings and concerns through concentrated respectful listening, being deeply present, then asking clarifying questions which support the child to come to her own conclusions. Companioning draws out the child's own resources.

Advice or rescue when children, or people of any age, are grappling with something meaningful literally de-means them and is, in a sense, a violation of their spirit. We have all been violated in this way. It leaves a thin film of shame over us, as if the other person is saying, "You are helpless. I am the helper. I know and you don't know." Children are remarkably resourceful given compassionate, detached listening with a few clarifying questions which help them to get perspective, first on what they are feeling and, second, what virtues apply to the situation.

The more "brilliant advice" parents offer, the more children turn off or shut down, particularly in adolescence, when they are so vulnerable and their moral choices are so compelling.

A fourteen-year-old girl had cried alone for several days and finally found the courage to speak to her father about something that was deeply troubling to her. She went to her father and said, "Dad, I don't know what to do. I'm so shy and self-conscious with other kids. What should I do?" Instead of acknowledging how painful these feelings were for her, her father thought for a moment and said, "Just stop being so self-conscious." She turned away, now feeling shamed and hopeless, and, without even knowing it, decided never to turn to her father again. He had closed the door.

There are seven facets which sometimes serve as steps in the process of spiritual companioning and sometimes can be used singly to respond with the attitude of a spiritual companion. The Art of Spiritual Companioning is about presence. It is very intimate, and yet it is the most respectful way to open a space to allow someone to bring the truth, their own truth, to light.

(See Appendix A, Discussion Exercise 13, "Spiritual Companioning with Children.")

Open the Door

When a child opens the door herself, as this young woman did by initiating the talk with her father, the parent needs to keep the door open by asking cup-emptying questions. Father could have asked, "What is that like for you?" and allowed her to talk and to cry. Sometimes you can see that a child is hurting or needing to talk, and you want to take the initiative. You need some door openers which are as open-ended as possible. Rather than asking questions with a predetermined answer such as "Are you having a good day?" or trying to second-guess them when they look sad and asking "Are you having a bad day?" a door-opener question is "What kind of a day are you having?" or "How are things going for you?" One father asks when he first sees his children in the evening, "So, what's new?" Remember to shield your heart with a veil of compassion and detachment. The veil of compassion allows your empathy to flow through, but the detachment keeps you from taking on your child's feelings. The key is not to overreact or underreact but to meet the other right where he is.

Offer Receptive Silence

Receptive silence gives others the space to speak fully, to tell you the whole story without interruption. When the person you are listening to begins to disclose, to talk of what she is feeling, give her your silence, your most receptive, respectful, compassionate, and detached silence. Concentrate fully, peacefully, in a spirit of trust in the other's process. Deep listening cannot occur in the presence of an agenda. Your purpose is to support, not to rescue or distract or advise. If you see your child, or anyone to whom you are listening, as a capable, spiritual champion learning her lessons, you will enjoy being a companion to her as she does her spiritual work. A First Nations woman in northern Canada gave spiritual companioning a nickname. "I can't remember those words you call it," she said, "but it sure works with me and my kids. I call it 'walk along.'"

How long should you remain silent? A young Maltese priest said, "When you think you have been silent long enough, be silent a little more." It is sometimes in the silence after someone has shared for a while that the truth dawns from within their awareness. The saying goes, "Don't just say something; stand there."

Ask Cup-Emptying Questions

Allow a person to empty his cup by asking cup-emptying questions that are open-ended and show the utmost non-judgmental curiosity. Use "what," "how," and "when" questions, not "who" and never "why." The reason for that is that when you ask someone, "Why do you feel sad?" it can feel like an interrogation, or a request for an instant analysis. We are famous for asking our children for an assessment of their behavior. "Why did you hit your brother?" What are we expecting, a thesis on sibling rivalry? When we ask "who" questions, such as "Who were you playing with when this happened?" it is information gathering so that we can make some kind of judgment. In companioning, you don't have to understand the details. You only have to be present to allow the other to hear himself.

Good cup-emptying questions can be very general, or they can zero in on the feelings the speaker has expressed. Take your cues from the speaker. Here are some examples of general questions intended to allow the child's cup to empty:

CHILD: I'm never going back to that stupid school.
PARENT: Oh?
CHILD: I hate school and I'm never going back.
PARENT: What do you hate about it?
CHILD: The teacher is mean and she doesn't like me.

50

PARENT: How is she mean? (*or:*) What gives you the feeling she doesn't like you?

CHILD: She's always yelling at me.

PARENT: How is that for you?

CHILD: Embarrassing. All my friends are watching.

Let the child fully express the experience, empty her cup before you companion her toward resolution. Sometimes the cup emptying will be the only thing you need to do. A parent can easily bypass the child's valuable emotional/spiritual process of discovering her own feelings and choosing how to act in light of those feelings. We minimize: "You know your teacher really likes you." We preach: "You don't have a choice. You have to go to school. Don't you want to get a good job?" We rescue, "Do you want me to talk to your teacher?" None of these responses gives the child an opportunity to discover her own resolution or to tap into her own virtues.

Cup-emptying questions can also be quite focused. One of the most effective cup-emptying approaches, once the child has named a feeling, is to ask a more focused question such as "What is the most difficult part of this?" or "What embarrasses you most when the teacher yells at you?" When someone is worried, ask, "What worries you the most?" or if the child says things like "I don't know what to do," ask "What is most confusing?" Children often say "I don't know." Try asking, "What don't you know?"

Asking, "What does it mean to you when . . . ?" helps a person to access the meaning of the situation so that he can then master both his feelings and his choices.

Focus on Sensory Cues

While someone is sharing, if anything arises that has to do with a visual image or one of the other senses, zero in on it. The perceptions of the body are a pathway to the truths of the soul. Focus on what he is seeing, hearing, sensing. For example, if a child is describing a terrifying nightmare of a scary monster with sharp teeth, rather than trying to reassure him with an invalidating remark like "You're safe, there aren't any monsters," respond precisely to what he has said. "Ooh. A scary monster with sharp teeth!" or you can ask, "What were those teeth like?" The child will then be able to release and discharge his fear or whatever emotion he is feeling. A child who has something coming up which will take courage is naturally going to feel some fear. That is a good time to offer companioning.

CHILD: I have a knot in my stomach. I'm so scared to go on stage today.
PARENT: What does the knot feel like?
CHILD: It's right here. (*moving hand around his abdomen*)
PARENT: (*looks at the spot with both compassion and detached curiosity—not a furrowed brow. Parent does not jump up for the Kao-pectate*) How big is it?
CHILD: It fills my whole stomach, and then it goes up my neck.
PARENT: Hmm. A big lump all the way up.

If the child loses interest in the conversation at this point, and he may, having emptied his cup somewhat, the parent can say something like, "Going on stage sounds scary. I admire your courage."

An important time to focus on perceptual cues is when a child is injured. Focus on the injury. "That's a real red bump you have." It may actually speed the healing process.

Reflect feelings, using key words used by the speaker, or focus in on the perceptual, physical cues. This is like a dance, and in the beginning you are definitely following the speaker's lead. The goal of spiritual companioning, whether offered to a child or an adult, is to listen them into their own clarity by giving them the chance to hear their own feelings and thoughts.

Ask Virtues-Reflection Questions

When a person's cup seems empty, give a few more moments of silence. There is a coffee slogan, "Good to the last drop." Sometimes the last drop contains the pearl of truth. When a person gets to the bottom of her cup, the truth is always found there. You have given her the opportunity to hear herself think and feel. At this point you as the listener begin to take more of the lead, but not with your agenda for how the story ends, only a desire to support the speaker to reflect on the virtues which can support her to act responsibly. You may not always go on to this aspect of companioning, but if you can detect a virtue that is involved, it is helpful to do so. Your goal here is to ask questions which help the other to choose how she is going to act in light of her feelings.

These questions will help the person to make moral choices based on her virtues. Examples are:

> To a child going on stage: "It seems quite scary to go on stage. What will give you the courage to do it?"
>
> To a child having problems in his relationship with his teacher: "How do you think that you can get some justice and respect from your teacher?"
>
> Only after a child has had a chance to reflect on the virtues involved, you may also want to ask, "What support do you need to find a peaceful solution with your teacher?" or "How can I support you?"

In a moral dilemma, such as a loyalty issue for a teenager who has witnessed a friend shoplifting, the last thing she needs is for you to take the issue away. "You'll never see that friend again, I can tell you." Don't tell. Ask. After the child has emptied her cup completely, including her confusion about what to do, don't jump into the breach and give her your moral solution. Ask her a virtues-reflection question to help her discover her own. "How can you be loyal to your friend and honest at the same time?" "What feels right to you?" Kids come up with amazingly honorable solutions when given a virtues-based frame of meaning within which to choose.

Ask Closure and Integration Questions

There are questions which allow for closure and internalizing of a teachable moment, and the integration—the weaving together—of thinking and feeling, head and heart. Here are some suggested questions:

> "What is clearer to you now?"
>
> "What is clearer after talking about this?"
>
> "What has been helpful about talking?"
>
> "What have you appreciated most about talking?"

These closure and integration questions would come after a relatively lengthy time of listening, when some real cup emptying has occurred, not necessarily after you have just admired a bump on a child's knee. They are very important to help a person reach closure and pull it all together when a moral issue or strong emotion is involved.

It is essential that the listener not have an agenda for what "the" right answer is. Children are particularly sensitive to manipulation by adults. The parent who has a pre-set answer or who comes up with a brilliant idea during the companioning must use detachment to hold back. To serve as a spiritual companion takes a great deal of trust in the child's process. Once a parent has experienced the exhilaration of watching a child come to his own creative solutions, it is far more comfortable to try again.

Offer Virtues Acknowledgments

Finally, end with a virtues acknowledgment. It is essential to do this step in order to restore the dignity and self-esteem of someone who has opened her heart and soul to you. "I see your courage." "Your friend is lucky to have you. You're being really faithful to her." "I honor you for your sense of justice and your trust to tell me what is happening with your teacher and for your courage to work it out with her."

Be careful not to label with the virtues. It is not appropriate to say, "You are so honest," "You have so much courage," or "You're the most honest person I know." The acknowledgment will be immediately rejected because the person may not always be so honest. The most powerful virtues acknowledgments are very specific and relevant to the issue at hand. When they ring true, they touch the soul.

In the role of counselor you have moved a step beyond serving as the teacher at teachable moments. You are the mentor and supporter empowering the child to be his own teacher. As you practice spiritual companioning, you will see what an art and skill it is. The biggest challenge is getting out of the way. You will also see that it is a tool needed in every relationship, whether marriage, management, friendship, or parenting. Beginning when children are small gives them a wonderful head start in their spiritual growth and self-esteem.

CHAPTER 3

How to Apply
The Family Virtues Guide
in Your Family

Introducing The Virtues Project
to Your Children

There are lots of ways to use the principles and strategies of The Virtues Project in your life and in your family. For some people, speaking the language of the virtues is enough to create an atmosphere of greater peace and kindness at home. Others may want to try some of the suggestions here as a way of helping your family to focus on one of the fifty-two virtues in *The Family Virtues Guide* on a weekly basis. You will discover the approach that works best given your own interests and the ages of your children. The following ideas are meant to help you get started. Please feel free to use whatever works for you and change the rest. Your own enthusiasm is what will carry the project in your household.

The Virtues Project is a program for personal and spiritual growth rather than a technique to be used just to change the behavior of children. Your willingness to set spiritual goals for yourself, such as a new habit of self-discipline in the way you do your work or care for your health or create time for reverence, will help your children to understand that the virtues are about real life. It is very important that you model honesty by being real when you take part in the sharing.

Suggestions for Getting Started

Set a Time to Meet

Invite your family to a gathering at a specific time, explaining that you will be sharing a new family activity you have learned about. Announce it in advance and arrange a time which is convenient for everyone. Don't reveal too much about it. Let some surprise build up.

Open with Something Simple and Reverent

This can be lighting a candle, saying a prayer, or putting *The Family Virtues Guide* on a lovely cloth. (See other suggestions on next page.)

Say some brief words of welcome, naming each person's name or have a simple prayer, such as "We are thankful to be together. Help us to open our hearts to new ideas and to support each other with love and respect."

Describe **The Family Virtues Guide**

Using words which fit your children's ages, tell them something brief. "I have been reading a wonderful book. People all over the world of all different colors, religions and countries are using it. Do you know why? It tells us what's good about us. It helps us to remember to be the best people we can be. It teaches us words about virtues. I would like to have us meet once a week to look at one of the virtues in this book and help each other to practice it."

If you have older children, for example, ages nine through fourteen, you may want to set a different tone. "I have discovered a book being used all over the world, to help families grow closer and to help each person in the family in their own personal growth. It's called *The Family Virtues Guide*. I would like to propose we meet for three weeks to choose a virtue each week, work on it in ourselves and support each other by sharing about it at the end of the week.

The Family Virtues Guide is about what's good about us. Let me give you an example." Then give virtues acknowledgments about a specific virtue you have observed in each person in the family, and ask one person to acknowledge a virtue in you. They can look at the fifty-two virtues on page 64.

Example: "John, I noticed your courage when you spoke to your teacher about that late assignment. Maria, you were being considerate when you helped me find my keys." Be sure to acknowledge the adults in the family as well. This is not something adults are "doing" to kids. "Grandma, I want to acknowledge you for your patience when we all got home so late for dinner on Tuesday after the game."

Set Clear Boundaries for a Sharing Circle

When your family is sharing about virtues, you need to practice some boundaries in the form of ground rules to keep it special. One way to do that is to establish a time during the meeting for a sharing circle. The boundaries for a sharing circle are:

Courtesy

We will treat each other as we wish to be treated. When we are sharing about our own virtues practice, there will be no cross talk, only courteous silence.

Respect

We will listen to one another in silence, being deeply present to each other without interrupting, criticizing, advising, or teasing.

Trustworthiness

We will keep everything someone says in this sharing time private. It is not okay to bring up anything anyone shares in this gathering later, unless that person gives permission to do so.

You may want to spend time in your first meeting making a boundaries poster and having each person contribute by coloring a border or cutting out magazine pictures which fit each boundary or drawing a picture to illustrate each boundary.

Choose a Virtue to Practice This Week

At this point, you need to model respect and unity by inviting everyone to express how they would like to do this, either by beginning with the first virtue in the guide or picking one that your family agrees is most needed. You may choose to have a silent vote by passing out bits of paper and having each one write his preference on it. Or it may work better to simply begin with the first virtue and work your way through all fifty-two.

When the virtue is chosen, read from each of the four pages on the virtue. Write the affirmation on a piece of paper and post it somewhere that everyone can see it. Explain that each of you will come to the family meeting next week and share your experiences of practicing this virtue and will acknowledge times you saw each other practicing the virtue.

An alternative way to choose a virtue to practice is to do a "virtues pick," having each person close their eyes and flip open *The Family Virtues Guide* to a virtue. That can be the virtue she practices for the next week (see Appendix D, page 318).

Practice Moderation

Don't go on too long even if people are really enjoying it. Close by asking a closure and integration question and going around the circle to hear each person's answer in turn. "What did you most appreciate about this meeting?" Be sure to share your own answer to that question when it is your turn. Then close with a simple ritual, such as a song, then everyone blowing out the candle and putting away the materials you have used.

How to Hold a Family Virtues Meeting

After your first meeting, it will be best if you decide on a simple format and keep to it, at least for a while. Here are some guidelines for a successful meeting:

Balance Creativity and Order

Have a chairperson to assure the boundaries are clear and are practiced. If necessary, have a brief time out established if someone fails to practice courtesy or respect. Invite the child back in after a very short time, asking "Are you ready to be courteous now?"

A Sample Agenda

The Chair is also responsible for keeping to a simple agenda and asking closure and integration questions. Here is a sample agenda:

1. Opening Ritual.
2. Sharing Circle.
3. Virtues Game.
4. Pick new virtue(s) for this week.
5. Have a discussion or role plays on the new virtue.
6. Write out the affirmation and post it.
7. Close with a ritual.

Keep It Positive

This is meant to be a positive time to come together to share progress in the development of the inner life, a safe time to share successes and challenges in practicing the virtues. To be successful, it must create an atmosphere reflective of courtesy, respect, and trust. Remind people of the boundaries and model them yourself. Don't use the family virtues meeting to air problems. Children would see it as a time when they can expect to be embarrassed rather than uplifted.

Keep It Simple and Sacred

Begin and end with a simple ritual which is meaningful to your family. Some ways that families do this are:

- Buy or make a special candle and light it each time you have a virtues gathering.
- Spread a lovely cloth or piece of fabric on the floor or on a low table and place *The Family Virtues Guide* on it.
- Sit in a circle on the floor with something in the center such as a bowl of flowers.

- Ask each person in the family to bring something they care about—a favorite teddy bear, a special book, a found treasure such as a stone or leaf, and place it inside the circle or on a cloth in the center of the circle.

Don't cram in other family business. Keep this gathering very purposeful.

Practice Reverence with a Sharing Circle

Spend at least a portion of the time in a sharing circle, with the boundaries in place to preserve the safety and trust, with each person taking a turn and being listened to in silence with no cross talk or interruption.

One way to keep the boundaries of the sharing circle is to pass a "talking stick" or feather as some indigenous people do. Only the person holding it may speak.

In the sharing circle, take turns telling of your successes with virtues or with the virtue of the week chosen last time. Here are some examples of ways to share the virtue you have been practicing:

MOTHER (as Chairperson): Let's begin our sharing circle by sharing a sign of success each of us had with our virtues. What did each of us feel best about in the way we practiced the virtue? When each person is finished speaking, the rest of us will give virtues acknowledgments. Shall I start?

I practiced moderation this week by taking some time out to read a new book. I'm pleased that I'm taking care of myself. Now, would you please tell me what virtues you noticed in me this week? *(Others acknowledge Mother for virtues they noticed in her.)*

ANNA *(age six)*: I was friendly. I met a new girl at school and asked her to sit with me to eat lunch. *(Virtues acknowledgments follow.)*

KARL *(age nine)*: My hamster didn't die. I was really glad. So, then I was prayerful because I said "Thanks, God."

FATHER: I rode my bike to work two days this week. I feel good about helping the earth by reducing the amount of gas I used. That was respect.

If you have all been focused on one virtue, the sharing circle is a time to share how it went for you, then give each other acknowledgments about times you noticed the virtue of the week being practiced.

60

Apply Creativity and Joyfulness

Have fun with the virtues! One activity enjoyed by children in families and schools of many countries is to role play the "What would it look like" situations on page three of the virtue, first without the virtue. Then, what would the situation look like if the virtue were being practiced. Have a dress up box with hats or other items to wear. Engage in the role play with your children.

You may want to make a virtues tree felt board and use it for role plays and stories. (See Appendix C for instructions.)

There are a number of games which can be adapted with virtues, such as "Virtues Charades" where each person does a simple gesture without speaking and the others guess what virtue they are portraying. Whoever is the first to guess correctly gets to do the next charade.

Another game is "Who Practiced the Virtue?" It is a form of musical chairs. Arrange chairs in a circle with people sitting in them. There should be a chair for each person except the leader. The leader stands and, having picked a virtue, asks "Who practiced cleanliness today?" Everyone must be honest and get up if they practiced this virtue, and they cannot sit back down in their own chair. The object is to find another chair, and the leader tries to find a chair to sit in. Someone is then left standing in the leader's place. That person says how he practiced the virtue today, then asks who practiced a different virtue. It is helpful to have a virtues poster to refer to. (See Appendix D re how to order a poster of the fifty-two virtues.)

Review the New Virtue of the Week

At this point you will want to choose a virtue and read what *The Family Virtues Guide* says about it. Adapt the length of your reading to the ages of the children.

Then follow the pattern you have chosen for focusing on that virtue. It could be:

- In sharing circle, each names a time you practiced this virtue.
- Name someone you know who practices this virtue and how you have noticed it in them.
- When it is each person's turn, the others can name a time they saw this person practicing the virtue.

Create Peacefulness with a Closing Ritual

Some of the ways families do this are:

- A final sharing circle with each person sharing "what I appreciated best about this meeting."
- Blowing out the candle.
- Singing a virtues song.
- Saying a prayer.

Choose a song you know and add virtues to it. One example is "Holy ground, we're standing on holy ground, for love (or other virtue) is present and where love is is holy." Or sing "Love is like a magic penny, hold on tight and you won't have any. Lend it, spend it, give it away and it comes right back to you." Then sing it a few times, substituting other virtues for the word "love."

Act with Tact

In the days between family virtues gatherings, be tactful in speaking the language of the virtues in teachable moments focused on the virtue picked for that week. Particularly be on the look-out for moments when you see someone in the family practicing the virtue and give a virtues acknowledgment.

If there is a teachable moment when someone is failing to practice the virtue, use a virtues-based approach to giving that person feedback. To act with tact, remember the letters A, C, and T. Acknowledge, correct, and thank. Here is an example of a child who has been forgetting to practice respect during the day. When you are saying goodnight or tucking him in say "Son, I want to give you some feedback on how I have noticed you practicing respect. First I acknowledge you for being respectful tonight when it was bedtime and you came right to bed. You were respecting the boundary about bedtime. Today, you needed more practice when you teased your sister, when you hit your friend, and when you spoke to me disrespectfully before dinner. I want to thank you for the respectful way you are listening to me right now." This may occasion a child talking about what went wrong. If so, companion him. Don't lecture. Don't preach. Listen.

SON: It was too hard to be respectful all day. I couldn't do it.

PARENT: What was too hard?

SON: I didn't feel like it.

PARENT: (*Nonjudgmental, attentive silence.*)

SON: I'm sorry, Mom.

PARENT: What are you sorry for?

SON: I'm sorry for forgetting to be respectful. I'll try harder tomorrow.

PARENT: You sound very purposeful. I know you can do it.

May your family gatherings be healing, unifying, and enjoyable.

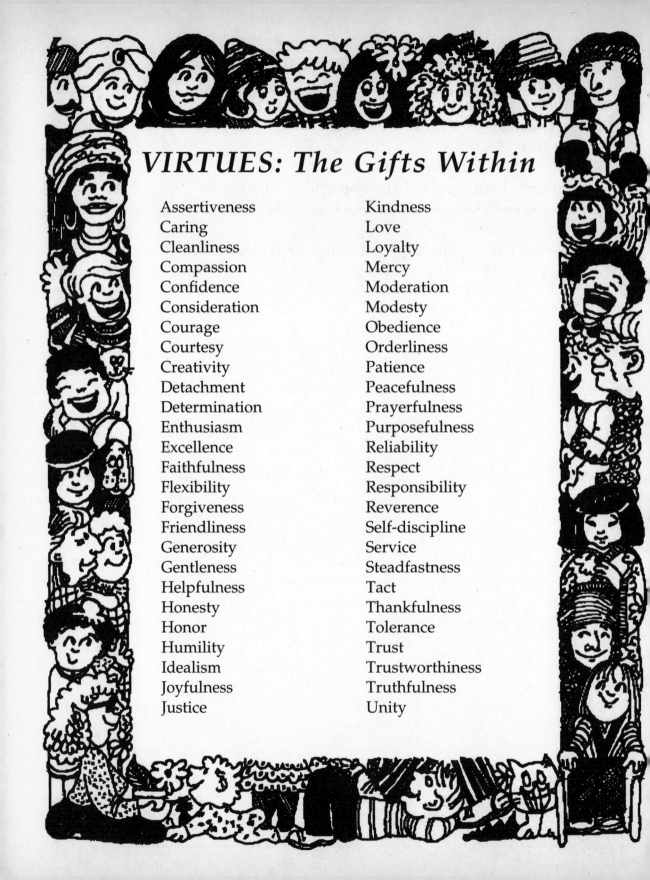

VIRTUES: The Gifts Within

Assertiveness	Kindness
Caring	Love
Cleanliness	Loyalty
Compassion	Mercy
Confidence	Moderation
Consideration	Modesty
Courage	Obedience
Courtesy	Orderliness
Creativity	Patience
Detachment	Peacefulness
Determination	Prayerfulness
Enthusiasm	Purposefulness
Excellence	Reliability
Faithfulness	Respect
Flexibility	Responsibility
Forgiveness	Reverence
Friendliness	Self-discipline
Generosity	Service
Gentleness	Steadfastness
Helpfulness	Tact
Honesty	Thankfulness
Honor	Tolerance
Humility	Trust
Idealism	Trustworthiness
Joyfulness	Truthfulness
Justice	Unity

❧ ASSERTIVENESS ❧

> *"Are not five sparrows sold for two small coins? Yet not one of them has escaped the notice of God. Even the hairs of your head have all been counted. Do not be afraid. You are worth more than many sparrows."*
>
> —LUKE 12:6–7

What Is Assertiveness?

Being assertive means to be positive and confident. It is knowing that you deserve respect. Assertiveness begins by being aware that you are a worthy person created by God. You have your very own special gifts. Only you have your unique combination of qualities.

When you are assertive, you tell the truth about what is just. You don't follow others. You think for yourself. If someone is trying to hurt you, lead you into trouble, or influence you to do something you feel is wrong, you protect yourself. You show the strength not to let others hurt you or influence you in negative ways.

Assertiveness is asking for what you want and need.

Assertiveness is expressing your own ideas, opinions, and talents. When you do this, you serve the world in your own special way. You are using the gifts God gave you.

Why Practice Assertiveness?

Without assertiveness we would be passive. We would let others boss us around. Without assertiveness we would just react to the things that other people expect of us. Others would tell us what to do and what to think. We wouldn't stop to figure out what we want, need, or think.

If you were too passive, you would allow others to hurt you or get you into trouble. You would not be able to set limits that keep you safe.

The trouble with being too passive is that your special way of being and thinking would remain unexpressed and the world would be a poorer place.

Without assertiveness you might be too aggressive. You would try to control others, push them around or hurt them. You would feel bad about yourself.

When you are assertive, others respect you. You are offering your true ideas and feelings as well as protecting yourself from things that can cause you harm. When you are assertive you choose what you will do for reasons of your own. God made you the way you are to play your special part in the world. Just as each instrument in an orchestra is needed to make beautiful music, your part is needed in the song of life.

How Do You Practice It?

To be assertive, you need to remember how worthy you are. You stand up for what you know is right. You don't allow others to treat you unjustly. You set limits with others by letting them know what you will and will not do. You listen to yourself and decide for yourself.

When you have ideas, you speak out, even if you feel shy. You are your own leader. Being assertive does not mean you control things or always get your own way. It means that when someone asks what you think or how you feel, you don't just tell them what they want to hear. You honestly and tactfully tell them what's true for you.

When someone suggests something that makes you feel uneasy, might hurt you or get you into trouble, you stop and think. You tell them you won't do it. You don't let other people bully or hurt you. You get help when you need it. You also avoid being aggressive. You don't need to hurt or boss others to feel important. You remember the one-of-a-kind unique combination that you are. The Creator wants you here as a blessing to the world.

What would assertiveness look like if . . .

- You start to feel inferior around some really popular kids?

- An aggressive child starts to bully you?

- Your teacher asks the class for their opinions about a story he has just read?

- A friend asks you to go somewhere you really don't feel like going?

- A group you are with tries to convince you to do something harmful?

Signs of Success

Congratulations! You are practicing assertiveness when you . . .

- Recognize you are worthy of respect

- Think for yourself

- Tell the truth about what is just

- Ask for what you want and need

- Set boundaries about what is right for you

- Freely express your thoughts and feelings

Keep trying! You need more practice when you . . .

- Forget that you are a person of value

- Let other people lead you into trouble

- Feel inferior to others

- Tell others only what you think they want to hear

- Are too passive

- Are too aggressive

⟫ AFFIRMATION ⟪

I am assertive. I think for myself and do what I feel is right. I tell the truth about what is just. I know I have the right to be treated with respect.

❧ CARING ❧

> *"Pay homage to God . . . and be good to your parents and relatives, the orphans and the needy and the neighbors who are your relatives, and the neighbors who are strangers, and the friend by your side."*
>
> —AL-QUR'AN, 4:36

What Is Caring?

Caring is giving love and attention to people and things that matter to you. You can show you care about someone by saying and doing things that help them. Caring about something you are doing means giving it your very best.

When you care for someone, you pay a lot of attention to them and take an interest in what is happening to them. Caring shows that something or someone really matters to you. You can care for yourself, for others, for a pet or a special thing. When you care for an animal, you watch over it and take good care of its needs.

When you are careful with something, you treat it gently and respectfully, making sure that you don't hurt it. When you do a careful job, you give it your very best effort.

Caring comes from within. It is a sign of love, respect, and concern. Caring people take the interests of others as their own. They do all that they can to show people that they are loved and valued.

Caring about yourself means that you treat yourself with the respect and concern that you deserve as a child of God.

Why Practice Caring?

Caring makes the world a better place to live in. Caring people help others feel less alone. They help people when they are hurt, or sick, or weak, not because they have to or because it is their job. They care because other people matter to them. Because they care, people can trust them. Caring people treat special things with extra concern and attention. Caring people treat everyone with the love, respect, and concern they deserve. Caring begins by loving and respecting yourself and others.

Without caring, nothing and no one matters. Everyone is alone. If someone is hurt or sick, no one will help unless she can make some money or take advantage of the person. Without caring, people would only do things for others because they expect something in return. People would become suspicious of each other. When people have an attitude of "I don't care," they do a sloppy or incomplete job. Sometimes that can be dangerous for people and the environment.

When you don't care about yourself, others get the impression that you don't matter very much. They start being careless with you too.

How Do You Practice It?

When you feel love and concern for others, look for ways to show your interest in them. Ask them questions about how they are, what they think and feel, like "What did you do today?" "How is your day going?" "Are you feeling better?" and "How can I help?"

When you are careful, you handle things with control and gentleness. When someone or something is entrusted to your care, you treat their trust as something sacred, giving your best and nothing but your best.

When you care about the things you do, you do them with enthusiasm and excellence, whether it is a job at home or an assignment for school.

When you care about yourself, you treat your body with respect, wear clean clothes, take a bath, and comb your hair. You take care of your needs. If you are lonely, you find a friend and spend some time. If you are hungry, you get something to eat. If you are sad, you have a little cry and then decide how you can make things better.

What would caring look like if . . .

- You are doing a chore for your family?

- You notice that one of your friends looks a bit sad?

- You come in from playing outside and start talking to your mother?

- It is your job to take care of the family pet?

- You feel upset about something that is hard to talk about?

- Your sister lends you something she really likes?

Signs of Success

Congratulations! You are practicing caring when you . . .

- Treat others and yourself with care

- Let people know that what they say is important by looking at them and listening closely

- Handle things carefully

- Be gentle and loving with anything or anyone placed in your care

- Treat your body with respect

- Work with enthusiasm and excellence

Keep trying! You need more practice when you . . .

- Act as if you don't care, as if nothing matters to you

- Ignore other people's needs

- Give less than your best to a job

- Treat things carelessly

- Ignore your own needs

- Let things placed in your care fend for themselves (even pets!)

❧ AFFIRMATION ❧

I care for others and myself. I pay loving attention to people and things I care about. I give my best to every job.

❧ CLEANLINESS ❧

> "*I*n every aspect of life, purity and holiness, cleanliness and refinement, exalt the human condition and further the development of man's inner reality. Even in the physical realm, cleanliness will conduce to spirituality."
> —SELECTED WRITINGS OF ABDU'L-BAHA

What Is Cleanliness?

Cleanliness means washing often, keeping your body clean, and wearing clean clothes. When you practice cleanliness you feel (and smell!) fresh. Cleanliness means keeping your room neat and clean. It means doing your share to help your family keep your home in order.

Cleanliness can be in your mind as well as your body. A clean mind means that you keep your thoughts on things which are good for you. You can "clean up your act" by deciding to change when you have done something you aren't proud of or when you have made a mistake. It is "wiping the slate clean" and starting over when you want to improve yourself. "Staying clean" also means keeping your body free of harmful drugs.

🌱 🌱 🌱

Why Practice Cleanliness?

Keeping yourself clean not only makes you feel good. It makes you nice to be around. When you brush your teeth you have a better chance of having healthy teeth. Maybe you won't have any cavities!

Cleanliness protects you from disease. Washing your hands after you go to the bathroom and before you eat keeps away germs that cause disease. Wearing clean clothing helps you look your best. When your home is clean, your mind feels clean and uncluttered too. You can find things more easily.

A mind filled with pure and positive thoughts keeps you feeling peaceful. Being willing to clean things up in your behavior, to fix your mistakes, gives you happiness inside. Other people find that they can trust you.

Without cleanliness people get diseases, spread them to others, and smell unpleasant. When your home is messy, you cannot find anything and you feel ill at ease. When your mind gets caught in unpleasant and troubling thoughts, you get confused. People who use harmful drugs mess up their brains and lose the ability to think clearly.

When you keep yourself and your surroundings clean, it keeps your spirit strong and peaceful.

How Do You Practice It?

At a simple level, cleanliness is washing daily and brushing your teeth. It is putting things away after you are finished using them and helping to keep your home in order.

At another level, it is straightening yourself out, bringing yourself back to your best. Cleanliness means to remove those things that result in "dis-ease"—things that interfere with your well-being.

When you feel the need, clean up your act. Besides cleaning your body, clean up your language. Straighten up your room and ask God to help you straighten up your life.

Notice when unpleasant or unwelcome thoughts are on your mind. Try to understand why they are there and then work to replace them with thoughts which are good for you.

Only put into your body things which will make you healthy, like nutritious foods and drinks. Avoid putting anything in your body which could harm you.

When you make a mistake, clean it up by deciding to change. Apologize if you need to and then start acting differently.

What would cleanliness look like if . . .

- You haven't been able to find your shoes for three days because your room is so messy?

- You play with a toy that has lots of pieces and then decide you feel like doing something else?

- You notice that unwelcome thoughts are sticking in your mind?

- It's time for bed and you're so sleepy, you don't feel like brushing your teeth?

- After dinner, the kitchen is all messed up. Your mom usually does the dishes and she looks really tired?

Signs of Success

Congratulations! You are practicing cleanliness when you . . .

- Keep your body fresh and clean

- Put things away after you use them

- Do your share to help keep your home clean and neat

- Put only healthful things in your body

- Use clean language

- When you make mistakes, clean them up

Keep trying! You need more practice when you . . .

- Start to look and smell dirty

- Forget about washing or brushing your teeth

- Leave things out instead of putting them away neatly

- Don't help with the family cleaning

- Keep living in the midst of clutter

- Use unclean language

- Keep making mistakes without trying to straighten them out

❧ AFFIRMATION ❧

I keep myself fresh and clean. I put my things and my life in order. With God's help I am able and willing to clean up any mistake.

❧ COMPASSION ❧

"He who is incapable of hatred toward any being, who is kind and compassionate, free from selfishness, . . . such a devotee of Mine is My beloved."
—BHAGAVAD-GITA 12: 13–14

What Is Compassion?

Compassion is understanding and caring about someone who is in trouble or has made a mistake. It is being kind and forgiving because another person really matters to you. It is feeling sorry when someone is hurt (it might be you) and needs someone to understand. It is forgiving someone who hurt you because you understand why they hurt you and care more about that person than your own hurt. It is feeling the pain of someone who is in trouble even if you do not know that person. It is caring deeply and wanting to help—even if all you can do is to listen and say kind words.

❧ ❧ ❧

Why Practice Compassion?

When people feel bad or find themselves in trouble, they usually feel very much alone. Feeling alone can make things even worse. At such times people start to believe that no one understands or cares about them at all.

Being compassionate tells a person that they are not alone. It makes you a friend when someone needs a friend. It gives you a good feeling and makes you useful at the same time. It helps you to understand other people and yourself.

Without compassion the world is a hard and lonely place. With compassion we are all connected and hard times are much easier because others understand and care.

How Do You Practice It?

Compassion begins by paying attention to yourself and to others. Notice when someone looks sad or is having some trouble in his life (it could be an animal or a person).

Go up to that person and show that you understand and care by:

- Sitting close by, letting him know that you are there and that he is not alone

- Listening if he wants to talk

- Sharing your own experience if you had a similar one

- Understanding and forgiving him if he hurt you without meaning to

- Doing what you can to help—it might just be praying for him

What would compassion look like if . . .

- Your dog is caught up in his leash?

- A friend is confused about what the teacher said?

- Someone is sad because her mother is sick in the hospital?

- A new student is lonely and feels left out?

- Your father seems very tired after work?

Signs of Success

Congratulations! You are practicing compassion when you . . .

- Notice when someone is hurting or needs a friend

- Care enough about her to stop what you are doing and let her know that you care

- Listen to her and try very hard to understand

- Forgive her when she hurts you and give her another chance to be a friend instead of hurting her back

- Help people and animals in need

Keep trying! You need more practice when you . . .

- Do not notice when you or the people and animals around you are sad or having trouble

- Think what you are doing is more important than what is happening to others

- Don't stop to listen or show you care

- Get bored or inattentive when others talk to you

- Judge or criticize others and yourself

- Hurt others back because you are angry

⊰ AFFIRMATION ⊱

I have compassion. I notice when someone needs attention and freely offer my help.

❧ CONFIDENCE ❧

> *"Do not, therefore, throw away your confidence, for it carries a great reward."*
> —HEBREWS 10:35

What Is Confidence?

Confidence is being certain and feeling assurance. It comes from knowing and trusting someone. Self-confidence means you trust yourself. You can do things without doubts holding you back. You know your strengths and weaknesses.

When you are confident in others, you rely on them and trust them. Confidence in God is a sense of trust that your Creator loves you and watches over you as you go through life.

Confidence brings peace of mind. When you are confident, you act with strength. You like to try new things. Confidence means that you don't allow fear or doubt to keep you from doing what you really want to do.

With confidence you feel certainty even when others try to confuse you or make you doubt. You do your best without worrying about what is going to happen. Instead of being afraid of failure, you have confidence that you can learn from your mistakes.

When you have confidence, you trust that whatever comes to you in your life is a gift from God for your perfecting.

Why Practice Confidence?

When you have confidence, you try new things and learn all the time. Without confidence, fears and doubts would hold you back. You would worry, worry, worry. You would miss a lot because you were afraid of making a mistake, as if somehow mistakes mean you aren't worthwhile.

Without confidence you feel confused or afraid of what might happen to you. Even if you know how to do something, your worries make you feel uncertain. Since you are worrying, you can't give things your best and they do not work as well.

Confidence gives you the ability to try new things and fail sometimes, knowing that you can learn from your mistakes. God brought us into this world not to show off how perfect we are, but to help us learn to perfect ourselves, step by step.

Confidence means that instead of being suspicious with others, you trust them unless you have a good reason not to. With confidence in God you know that everything that happens to you will work out for the best if you learn from it.

How Do You Practice It?

You practice confidence by knowing that you are worthwhile whether you win or lose, succeed or fail. You see yourself as a learner, and you welcome new experiences and new possibilities. You think positively. When fears come, you feel them, but you don't let them control what you do.

You watch yourself without judging. You don't criticize yourself harshly when you do something you are sorry for or make a mistake. You do what you can to correct it. You trust God to forgive you and help you to change.

You have self-confidence when you are able to try new things, watching yourself closely to see what works and doesn't. Then you try again, making little changes so it will turn out better next time.

Confidence in others is trusting them to do what they say they will do. Confidence in life means to trust that all things work together for good.

What would confidence look like if . . .

- Your friends invite you to play a game you have never played before?

- You are asked to speak in front of your class?

- You try out for a sport and don't get picked?

- You start to worry about performing in a play opening night?

- You did something that really upset your mother?

- You received a very low score on a math test?

Signs of Success

Congratulations! You are practicing confidence when you . . .

- Remember that you are worthwhile whether you succeed or fail

- Are willing to try new things

- Discover your talents

- Watch yourself without judging

- Learn from your mistakes

- Think positively

Keep trying! You need more practice when you . . .

- Are afraid to try new things

- Try impossible things

- Hide mistakes and don't try to learn from them

- Don't figure out how to make something work better

- Just do things without figuring out how to do them first

- Feel afraid, worried, or upset a lot of the time

❧ *AFFIRMATION* ❧

I am confident. When I try something new, I give it my best effort. I am free of worry. I welcome new possibilities and trust God to support me.

❧ CONSIDERATION ❧

> *"Let them at all times concern themselves with doing a kindly thing for one of their fellows, offering to someone love, consideration, thoughtful help."* —SELECTIONS FROM THE WRITINGS OF ABDU'L-BAHA

What Is Consideration?

Consideration is having regard for other people and their feelings. It is thinking about how your actions affect them and caring about how they feel.

Consideration is thoughtfulness. It is paying attention to what other people like and don't like, then doing things that give them happiness.

Consideration is giving the same importance to others' likes and dislikes as you do to your own. When you have different tastes, consideration means you don't try to convince other people that they are wrong and you are right. You respect their feelings. Consideration is giving thought to the needs of others.

❧ ❧ ❧

Why Practice Consideration?

When people behave selfishly and don't practice consideration, it hurts other people's feelings. When we are inconsiderate, others tend to be inconsiderate too. We might play our music so loud that it upsets people, or leave things lying around that can pose a danger.

Without consideration people get into arguments, because they feel their needs are being ignored. When you are considerate, things are more peaceful.

When you are considerate, people know that they are important to you because you consider them before you do things and check to make sure that things are all right afterward. When you practice consideration, others start to practice it as well. It's contagious!

How Do You Practice It?

Consideration begins by noticing how your actions are affecting other people. You find out what they like and don't like and then consider their feelings.

When you are considerate, you act as if others are just as important as you are. Consideration is asking yourself things like "Will this hurt or disturb someone else?" If the answer is yes, think of creative ways to do what you want and at the same time respect other people's rights.

Walk quietly when someone is reading. Wait to ask a question if someone is busy. Arrange your schedule to have dinner with your family or to be there in time to feed your pets.

To be considerate, give some thought to what would bring others happiness. When you want to give someone a gift, think really carefully about what would please that person. If someone is ill, bring him a drink or cover him with a blanket. Give him some loving attention. If someone is sad, put yourself in his position and think about what you would need from a friend.

What would consideration look like if . . .

- Your brother is feeling bored because he is sick and has to stay in bed?

- You and your parents have very different tastes in music and the volume it should be played?

- Your best friend is having a birthday?

- You're entering the front door at school and realize someone is right behind you?

- You have just come home from school and your grandmother is taking a nap?

Signs of Success

Congratulations! You are practicing consideration when you . . .

- Respect other people's needs and feelings

- Feel that other people's views are as important as your own

- Stop and think about how your actions will affect others

- Are quiet when people are concentrating or sleeping

- Put yourself in other people's shoes

- Give tender attention

- Think of little things which bring others happiness

Keep trying! You need more practice when you . . .

- Act without thinking about how other people will be affected

- Don't know what bothers people until they get mad

- Do things just the way you want to. Expect others to adjust if they don't like it

- Believe that only your feelings matter

- Ignore or forget birthdays and other gift-giving times

❈| *AFFIRMATION* |❈

I am considerate of others. I think about how my actions affect them. I think of thoughtful things which bring happiness to others.

❧ COURAGE ❧

*"**B**e strong, and let your heart take courage,*
All ye that wait for the Lord."—PSALMS 31:25

What Is Courage?

Courage is personal bravery in the face of fear. It is doing what needs to be done even when it is really hard or scary. Courage is going ahead even when you feel like giving up and quitting. Sometimes courage means recognizing a danger and standing firm. It doesn't mean taking unnecessary chances just to look brave.

Courage is needed in trying new things, in facing difficult situations, and in picking yourself up after a mistake and trying again. It is doing what you know is right even if other people laugh at you or call you names.

Courage is a quality of the heart. Courage comes from what you feel in your heart rather than just what you think. It comes from knowing yourself and knowing down deep that you can and should do something. Courage comes from knowing that God is there to help and that you can count on God always.

Love can give us courage. It gives us strength and helps us do the right thing without letting our fears stop us.

Why Practice Courage?

Courage is the best thing you can have when you are scared or unsure. There are times when you are not sure that you can do something. You might feel alone, facing what seems to be an impossible situation. Courage helps you do great things.

Without courage everyone would do only what is easy. No one would try new things that seem hard. Everyone would do what everyone else is doing, to avoid standing out—even if they knew it was wrong. Fear would be in charge. People would avoid anything that seemed hard.

How Do You Practice It?

You do what you know is right even when it is hard or scary. You face your mistakes with courage, learn from them, and keep trying. You try new things, like learning to ride a bike, even if it feels like you'll never learn.

You work to understand something which you are afraid of and decide if it is real or just imagined. Remember that you can always ask for help when you need it. You can count on God and others to give you strength and help.

You stand up for what you know is right even if all your friends are doing something wrong. You let courage fill your heart even if others laugh at you or call you names.

When you feel afraid, go ahead and feel your fear. Name it, then let it go. Decide what is the wise and courageous thing to do. Go ahead and do it even if you still feel afraid.

What would courage look like if . . .

- You are asked to speak in front of your class in school?

- All your friends want you to try something, like stealing or smoking, and you feel it is wrong?

- You see another child being teased and hurt by a group of children?

- You do something you are sorry for, like breaking one of your mother's favorite plates? No one knows who did it.

- You feel scared of the dark when you're trying to go to sleep? (What help do you need?)

Signs of Success

Congratulations! You are practicing courage when you . . .

- Do what you know is right even when it is hard or scary

- Admit mistakes and learn from them

- Are willing to try new things

- Ask for help from God and others

- Find courage in your heart even if others laugh at you or call you names

- Go ahead and do something you want to do even if you still feel afraid

Keep trying! You need more practice when you . . .

- Avoid doing new things for fear of failing

- Pretend you're not afraid

- Are afraid to admit your mistakes

- Do what everyone else does even if you know it is wrong

- Do the easy thing and not the right thing

- Think you can do everything yourself and not ask others (or God) for help when you need it

❧ AFFIRMATION ❦

I have the courage to try new things. I admit my mistakes and learn from them. I listen to my heart. I have the courage to do what is right.

COURTESY

"O people of God! I admonish you to observe courtesy, for above all else it is the prince of virtues. Who is endued with courtesy hath indeed attained a sublime station."
—Writings of Baha'u'llah

What Is Courtesy?

Courtesy is to be polite and to have good manners. It is to be considerate of others and to have gracious ways. It is a way of acting with people which makes them feel valued, cared for, and respected. Courtesy is something people use when they are trying to make a good impression. It's important to show courtesy with friends and relatives, not just people we are meeting for the first time.

"Please," "Thank you," "Excuse me," and "You're welcome" are not just words. They are courteous expressions which let people know you appreciate them and care about their feelings. Being courteous by not interrupting someone while they are speaking tells them that what they are saying is just as important as what you have to say. Being polite to your parents, elders, and teachers is especially important. It shows them that you respect them.

🌱 🌱 🌱

Why Practice Courtesy?

Practicing courtesy makes every person feel important and acknowledged. No one feels taken advantage of or insulted. The next time they come in contact with you, they want to be around you and to help you. Courtesy is like a magnet. It makes you attractive to others.

When a person doesn't practice courtesy, people feel insulted and assume that the person is ignorant. They get the impression the person just doesn't care about anyone or anything. Rude people are avoided. Others don't feel appreciated. They want to stay away.

How Do You Practice It?

You practice courtesy by learning polite ways to speak and then using them throughout each day. Instead of interrupting someone, you say, "Excuse me," and then wait patiently for them to give you their attention.

Courtesy means to think of how your behavior is affecting others and then do things properly so that they are comfortable: eating without showing the food in your mouth (ugh!); holding the door for someone who needs help; making requests by saying "please" instead of ordering someone to do something *now;* saying "thank you" and smiling when someone has done something for you. Courtesy is to look at someone you are meeting for the first time, smile, and say, "Hello." You may want to shake hands too.

Courtesy in school means listening to your teacher when she is speaking, stopping what you are doing when she asks you to, and being considerate with your classmates. Courteous people don't shove others out of the way to get in line first. They use their quiet voices indoors and save their loud voices for outdoors. There are lots of opportunities every day to practice courtesy.

What would courtesy look like if . . .

- You are meeting someone for the first time?

- Your parents are having a conversation and you want to speak to one of them?

- You are at a birthday party and the cake is being served?

- You answer the phone and the caller asks to speak to your sister?

- You have just walked into a worship service?

Signs of Success

Congratulations! You are practicing courtesy when you . . .

- Treat others as if you value and respect them

- Think about how your actions affect others

- Remember to treat elders, parents, and teachers politely

- Eat, speak, and move graciously

- Make requests instead of demands

- Greet people with a smile

Keep trying! You need more practice when you . . .

- Treat others rudely, or as if they don't matter

- Put yourself before others

- Forget to say "please," "thank you," "hello," and other expressions of courtesy

- Don't say anything when you meet new people

- Interrupt

- Push, shove, or act piggy when you eat

- Make demands instead of requests

- Answer the phone rudely

❧ *AFFIRMATION* ❧

I am courteous. I remember my manners and treat people with respect. I greet others politely. I show people that I care.

❧ CREATIVITY ❧

"Let us use the different gifts allotted to each of us by God's grace." —ROMANS 12:6

What Is Creativity?

You are a new creation. No one has ever been born who is just like you, with your special combination of gifts and talents. Creativity is a way to use your gifts to bring new things into the world. Creativity is a way to use the spark of God within you.

Creativity is expressing new ideas and inventions, new kinds of music, dance, and art. It is a way to let the light of originality within you shine out for the benefit of others. Creativity connects us with beauty.

Creativity is the power of imagination. It is seeing old things in new ways, doing things in a way that has not been done before.

❧ ❧ ❧

Why Practice Creativity?

Without creativity there would be no advancement in the world. Things would just stay the same. Without great ideas there would be no new inventions. We would just keep doing things as they have always been done. We would still be just riding donkeys to get somewhere instead of taking a plane, train, boat, or car.

Without music, art, and literature, life would be dull and boring. Listening to beautiful music uplifts people's souls. Wonderful dances, paintings, sculpture, and drawings have the same effect. When artists create, they bring joy to the world.

When we share our ideas with one another, things can be improved. When scientists are creative, they come up with new cures for diseases.

Every person can serve the world by learning about arts and sciences. We please our Creator when we practice the gift of creativity in our lives.

How Do You Practice It?

You practice creativity by developing your gifts to the fullest.

First, find out what they are. Notice what you like to do. Take time for dreaming. Then learn how to develop your gifts and talents so that you will get better and better.

Creativity is discipline in the service of vision. When you have a vision of something you want to create, you need to make it real. It could be a story, painting, dance, song, or new invention. Learning how to draw, or to play an instrument, or taking dance lessons, gives you the discipline to be creative.

Creativity is also working in a bakery and producing bread that tastes especially good. It is doing the familiar a little better than before. Creativity leads to an improvement.

Practicing creativity means doing things your own way rather than copying other people. Creativity is a way to use what the Creator has given you to serve the world.

What would creativity look like if . . .

- You wish you could play in the school orchestra?

- You get an idea for designing a new toy?

- The method you use to clean up your room takes too long?

- You wonder if you could write a poem?

- A friend is having a birthday party and you don't want to spend a lot of money on a gift?

Signs of Success

Congratulations! You are practicing creativity when you . . .

- Discover your gifts

- Use knowledge and training to develop them

- Think of new ways to make things work better

- Use your imagination

- Do things in your own, unique way

- Take time for dreaming

Keep trying! You need more practice when you . . .

- Don't believe you have any special gifts

- Leave your gifts undeveloped

- Don't use discipline when studying a science or art

- Do things the way you have always done them

- Just copy other people

- Use your talents only for yourself

❧ *AFFIRMATION* ❧

I am an original creation. I have special gifts and I am willing to discover them. I take time for inspiration. I think of new and better ways to do things. I am happy to be myself.

❧ Detachment ❧

*"**P**erform all thy actions with mind concentrated on the Divine, renouncing attachment and looking upon success and failure with an equal eye. Spirituality implies equanimity."*
—BHAGAVAD-GITA 2:47–48

What Is Detachment?

Detachment is experiencing your feelings without allowing your feelings to control you. It is choosing how you will act in a situation rather than just reacting. Feelings like sadness, happiness, disappointment, joy, frustration, anger—are natural. Everyone has them. Detachment is a way to use thinking and feeling together so that you don't let your feelings run away with you.

Detachment does not mean you pretend to feel differently than you do. Some people think detachment is being cold or pretending not to care, but when they try it, they find it is a joyful experience. Feelings are wonderful when they belong to us, when we use them to do what we really choose to do.

Detachment means to feel what you feel but not have to act on the feeling unless you want to. It's kind of like standing beside yourself and watching what you are feeling as well as feeling it.

Why Practice Detachment?

Detachment is very important for a spiritual being. It allows you to choose the way you are going to act no matter how you feel. It permits you to be kind to people you do not like, or do a very hard thing because it is the right thing to do.

Detachment helps you to decide what to do about strong feelings like anger. You can decide to use your voice to tell someone how mad you are and why rather than picking up the nearest object and slamming them with it!

Detachment can give you self-confidence. It is like going to a calm, peaceful place within your mind and looking at what is happening without getting swept away.

Without detachment you never know what you're going to do—it depends on how you feel! When you practice detachment a lot, it becomes easier to do, even when your emotions are very strong. Prayer and meditation can be a big help in learning detachment.

Without detachment you would stay away from all the things you don't like or which are hard to do—even if it is very important for you to do them. With detachment you can choose to do something you like in moderation rather than eating too much or playing a game too much and neglecting other things you need to do.

How Do You Practice It?

You can practice detachment whenever you have a feeling about something or someone. First you recognize the feeling—how can you be detached if you do not know what you are detached from? Stop and look at your feelings and thoughts. Ask yourself two questions:

- What am I feeling about this?

- What do I want to do?

Now pay attention to what you want to do. Ask yourself . . .

- Is it good for me?

- Will it help someone else?

- Is it right?

- Is it the best I can do?

If the answer to any of these questions is no, then choose to do something else instead.

Look. Choose. Act.

What would detachment look like if . . .

- Your mother asked you to do some chores and you feel like playing video games instead?

- Your sister takes your best sweater without asking and you feel really mad?

- You urgently want to win a game or join a team and it doesn't happen?

- Some children tease you in school?

Signs of Success

Congratulations! You are practicing detachment when you . . .

- Take time out before doing something you will be sorry for

- Look at your feelings before deciding how to act

- Use thinking and feeling together

- Pray or meditate before taking action

- Choose to do what is right

Keep trying! You need more practice when you . . .

- Ignore your feelings

- Do not know what you are feeling

- Automatically act on your feelings without thinking

- Think you are helpless when strong feelings come

- Do not decide what you want to do or say

- Lose your temper

❧ *AFFIRMATION* ❧

I am aware of my feelings and choose my actions with detachment. I do what is right for me. I choose to be my best self no matter what happens.

❧ DETERMINATION ❧

> "*They must be constantly encouraged and made eager to gain all the summits of human accomplishment, so that from their earliest years they will be taught to have high aims, to be of powerful resolve and firm of purpose in all things.*"
> —SELECTIONS FROM THE WRITINGS OF ABDU'L-BAHA

What Is Determination?

Determination is focusing your energy and efforts on a particular task and then sticking with it until it is done. Determination is using your willpower to do something even when it isn't easy.

When you are determined to do something, you know that it is very important. Determination means you care about doing something so much that even when it is really hard, or you are being tested, you still keep going.

🌱 🌱 🌱

Why Practice Determination?

Without determination many things don't get done. When it becomes difficult, people who are not determined give up. When they need help, they don't get help. They just stop.

Without determination people would wait and wait or depend on someone cheering or pushing them in order to get anything done. Without determination important things can be neglected.

When people are determined, even the hardest thing becomes a challenge they are willing to accept. They get important things done. They grow strong. They do things which matter in the world.

How Do You Practice It?

You practice determination by first deciding what is important to you. Then use your willpower to make it happen. You finish what you start. You deal with anything that gets in your way, and then you go back to what you were doing. You keep going even if something starts to distract you. You stay on purpose.

You get help when you need it because what you are doing is too important to give up on. If the way you are doing something is not working for you, figure out how to change things. When you get sad or discouraged, stop for a moment. Think about what you need in order to meet your goal. Then start again.

It feels good when you meet your goals.

What would determination look like if . . .

- You are trying to learn to ride a bike?

- You are doing a really hard homework assignment and it's due tomorrow?

- You are building a model for your dad's birthday and it gets pretty complicated?

- You decide to work on a new virtue and keep slipping into your old habits?

Signs of Success

Congratulations! You are practicing determination when you . . .

- Believe what you are doing is important

- Set goals for yourself

- Focus your attention on what you are doing

- Resist being distracted

- Keep going even if it gets difficult

- Ask for help when you need it

- Finish what you started

Keep trying! You need more practice when you . . .

- Believe what you are doing doesn't really matter

- Decide that you can only try

- Procrastinate

- Stop when things get difficult

- Fail to ask for help when you need it

- Don't finish what you set out to do

❈ *AFFIRMATION* ❈

I have determination. I set goals and keep going until I achieve them. I get things done. I stay on purpose.

❧ ENTHUSIASM ❧

"If you give to charity, give without grudging; if you are a leader, lead with enthusiasm; if you help others in distress, do it cheerfully." —ROMANS 12:8

What Is Enthusiasm?

Enthusiasm is being cheerful and happy. Enthusiasm is doing something wholeheartedly, with zeal and eagerness. It is giving a hundred percent to what you do, holding nothing back. Being enthusiastic is being excited about something, looking forward to it.

Enthusiasm means "God within." It is being filled with a positive spirit. It is not something you do but the way you go about doing it. You can be enthusiastic about going to school, taking out the garbage, or going fishing.

Enthusiasm is when you bring cheerfulness to whatever you do and give it your best. Enthusiasm makes even the dullest job fun.

❧ ❧ ❧

Why Practice Enthusiasm?

Enthusiasm is catching. When you are enthusiastic, other people get caught up in your excitement. Even the dullest job goes quickly. You find it easier to do your best because you are putting everything that you have into what you are doing. People like to be around you and to have you near them. Enthusiasm makes everyone's life more enjoyable.

Without enthusiasm things go slowly and are not much fun. There is no excitement, no passion. People who lack enthusiasm are passive. They hold back, do things grudgingly, and do not give their all.

If you lacked enthusiasm, you wouldn't get things done as well. People would accuse you of having an "attitude problem." Friends wouldn't want to be with you as much. They might start to avoid you.

Everything becomes boring to a person without enthusiasm. A person without enthusiasm becomes boring too.

How Do You Practice It?

Enthusiasm is an attitude. It comes from inside. You let yourself get excited about what you are doing and what you are planning. You become enthusiastic by thinking about how enjoyable something is going to be or thinking of ways to make it fun.

You cannot make yourself excited about everything, but you can help by using abilities you have within you. You can use your imagination to find the excitement in the things you do. You can think of new and original ways to do it.

Another way is to picture the results of what you do before they happen. If you are cleaning out a shed, picture what it will look like when you are done. Imagine how pleased people will be when they see it neat and clean.

Enthusiasm is taking time for simple pleasures and enjoying the wonders of life. You can show your enthusiasm toward others too, by celebrating with them when something wonderful happens. You show enthusiasm in your smile, the excitement on your face, saying things like, "Wow!" "This is great!" Showing your feelings of enthusiasm gives other people encouragement.

What would enthusiasm look like if . . .

- You particularly like a dish your mother or father cooked?

- You like a new song your friend played for you?

- Your sister did well in sports?

- You have a science project to do for school?

- You look outside one night and see the stars?

- You have a big chore to do for the family?

Signs of Success

Congratulations! You are practicing enthusiasm when you . . .

- Let yourself enjoy looking forward to something

- Give a hundred percent to what you are doing

- Think positively—look on the bright side of things

- Smile, laugh, and enjoy what you do

- Think of imaginative ways to get things done

- Enjoy the wonders of life

Keep trying! You need more practice when you . . .

- Keep cool—refusing to be excited about anything

- Hold back when you do things

- Get bored a lot

- Think negatively—look on the dark side of things

- Frown, complain, and have a miserable time while you do things

⊰| *AFFIRMATION* |⊱

I am full of enthusiasm. I give a hundred percent to whatever I do. I use my imagination. I am open to the wonders in store for me today.

❦ EXCELLENCE ❦

"In every art and skill, God loveth the highest perfection."

—BAHA'U'LLAH, BAHA'I
COMPILATION ON EXCELLENCE

What Is Excellence?

Excellence is doing your best. It is giving your best to any task you do or any relationship you have. Within you are many possibilities. Maybe you are an artist. Maybe you can discover a new invention that no one has ever created before. Maybe you are the best friend anyone will ever have. Perhaps there is some difficulty in your life which you have the strength to conquer.

When you practice excellence, you are not trying to be better than anyone else. You are trying to be the best that *you* can be.

No matter what you are doing, excellence means you are giving it the best you have. Excellence is effort guided by a noble purpose. It is a desire for perfection. The perfection of a seed is the fruit which grows from it. Excellence in your life is bringing your gifts to fruition.

❦ ❦ ❦

Why Practice Excellence?

Excellence is what leads to success. It takes courage to practice excellence. People who are afraid to find out if they are going to succeed or fail sometimes don't try very hard. If something doesn't turn out well, they say, "It doesn't matter. I wasn't doing my best anyway."

But they never find out what is really possible.

People who don't practice excellence just do things halfway. They try a little and then give up. Usually they don't have very exciting or fruitful lives. They act as if nothing matters very much—as if *they* don't matter very much.

When you practice excellence, you can break new ground and try new things that have never been thought of before. Doing your best helps you find out what talents you have, the special gifts God gave you. Doing your best helps you find out who you really are.

When you practice excellence, you can make a difference in this world.

How Do You Practice It?

Practicing excellence is doing your best with big things and little things, with the jobs you do and the people you love. It is striving to do today what you found difficult yesterday. It is the willingness to learn from your mistakes.

Excellence means you are not content with giving less than what you are capable of giving. It is making sure that when you do a job, you pay careful attention to it and don't leave it half done. If you find you are unable to do something, find something else which is possible for you to do. You are not meant to do everything well. Different people have different abilities. Choose what is right for you and then do it with as much enthusiasm, creativity, determination, and joy as possible.

Striving for excellence isn't always about doing. It is also about being. You need excellence when you are working on a virtue, like patience or honesty. Excellence comes as you pay careful attention, as you improve little by little, day by day. That is how a tiny seed grows into a giant tree. That is how your hidden gifts can bear fruit in the world.

What would excellence look like if . . .

- You're cleaning your room?

- You're learning something new, such as playing an instrument?

- You feel as if nothing you try is successful?

- You get tired in the middle of a job?

- You start comparing yourself to others?

- You discover that you have made too many promises or have too much to do?

Signs of Success

Congratulations! You are practicing excellence when you . . .

- Give your best to whatever you do

- Give your best to relationships

- Set noble and realistic goals for yourself

- Remember to plan and practice

- Don't try to do everything

- Develop your own gifts

Keep trying! You need more practice when you . . .

- Start something new without a plan

- Try to be all things to all people

- Try to do too much—or settle for too little

- Are afraid to fail

- Belittle your own gifts

- Quit before you are finished, or when you could do more, or better

❧ *AFFIRMATION* ❧

Today I thank God for my gifts. I will give my best to the work I do and be at my best with others. I dare to set noble goals, to do what is possible. I choose excellence in all things.

❧ FAITHFULNESS ❧

"Be faithful till death, and I will give you the crown of life." —JOHN 2:10

What Is Faithfulness?

Faithfulness is being true to someone or something. It is holding to what you believe is important no matter what happens. Faithfulness is belief that stands up to the test of time. It is starting out on a path and staying on it no matter how many times you stop or get distracted.

Faithfulness is being like a rock in the midst of rushing waters. You stand firm no matter what. It comes from really knowing and living what you believe. When you are faithful you can be counted on and trusted. You show up when you said you would show up. You keep your commitments regardless of what you would rather do.

Faithfulness is needed when you have beliefs and principles that can't be proven to others. If you are faithful to your beliefs, such as belief in God, honesty, or friendship, others can see your values in the way you act.

Why Practice Faithfulness?

When people don't show faithfulness, they say one thing and do another. One day they believe something, and the next day they believe something else. You never know what they believe. They probably don't know what they believe either. You can never count on them for anything. They say they will be somewhere, but then if something distracts them, they don't show up. They change their minds a lot. You never know where they stand. So people stop trusting them.

When people are faithful, you know what they stand for and you can trust them. You see their beliefs in their lives. You can count on them to keep their agreements. When people are faithful, they get things done regardless of the distractions that come up. They are faithful friends.

Once a friend, always a friend.

How Do You Practice It?

Being faithful means you keep your promises. You only make agreements you can keep. You walk your talk. If you say you will do something for someone else, you do it even if you feel like doing something else instead.

To do a job faithfully means you do it with as much excellence and precision as you can. And you do it on time.

You practice faithfulness by learning and questioning and finding answers about your beliefs. As you grow in your beliefs, you practice them as faithfully as you can.

Listen to your heart when things come up to test your faith. Faith is not really faith unless it is tested. Your faith gets stronger when your beliefs are tested and you still find that they are true.

When you are faithful in relationships, you are loyal. You don't talk about someone behind their back. If you feel mad or hurt, you go to them and talk about it privately. You don't leave an old friend when a new one comes along.

You make the circle wider.

What would faithfulness look like if . . .

- You told your father you would come right home but you are tempted to go with your friends to do something fun?

- You feel some doubt in your beliefs because people you admire don't agree with them?

- A new friend tries to get you to give up an old one?

- You have some homework to do and don't feel like doing the whole thing?

- You agreed to do a chore for your family every Saturday?

Signs of Success

Congratulations! You are practicing faithfulness when you . . .

- Listen to your heart when your beliefs are tested

- Only make promises you can keep

- Make sure your words and deeds match

- Keep your agreements

- Do a job as carefully and fully as it needs to be done

- Are loyal to your friends and family

- Clear up problems face to face

Keep trying! You need more practice when you . . .

- Don't believe that anything is important

- Accept a belief without thinking for yourself

- Change your beliefs if they are tested

- Say one thing and do another

- Talk about people behind their backs

- Don't keep your commitments

- Do a quick or sloppy job

❧ AFFIRMATION ❦

I am faithful to what I believe. I am a faithful friend. I do not backbite. I clear up problems face to face. I keep my promises. I walk my talk.

⊰ FLEXIBILITY ⊱

> "*Make me a tender herb in the meadows of Thy grace, that the gentle winds of Thy will may stir me up and bend me into conformity with Thy pleasure, in such wise that my movement and my stillness may be wholly directed by Thee.*"
>
> —WRITINGS OF BAHA'U'LLAH

What Is Flexibility?

Flexibility is being open to the need for change. Many unexpected things happen to us. We cannot control the things that happen. When upsetting things happen, this can be a message that we need to do things differently or improve ourselves in some way. Being flexible means that instead of just getting upset, you see difficulties as a challenge. You are willing to make necessary changes.

Flexibility means not always having to have your own way. You are open to the opinions and feelings of others. With flexibility you are willing to change your mind. If something doesn't work, you try a new way.

Flexibility means getting rid of bad habits and learning new ones. You look honestly at yourself and decide if you need to change the way you are acting.

Making changes doesn't mean you are losing yourself, only that you are becoming better.

Why Practice Flexibility?

When you are flexible, you adjust and adapt. You keep making positive changes. When you are open to change, you can accomplish more. Instead of doing things the same old way, you think of new and better ways to do them.

When things get tough, flexible people bend and become stronger. They keep learning and growing.

When people have a hard time being flexible, they keep doing things the same old way when new ways are needed.

When we don't practice flexibility, we become rigid. We get angry and upset when things don't go our way or when they don't happen as we expected.

People who have no flexibility don't like surprises.

How Do You Practice It?

Flexibility begins by recognizing a need to change something in yourself. It could be how you get things done or the need to acquire one of the virtues. If something in the way you act isn't working for you, this is probably a sign that there is a need for change. If something keeps going wrong in an area of your life, this may be a test which you need to accept and embrace. It could be teaching you what is next for you in your spiritual growth.

Once you *see* the need to change, *want* to change, and *decide* to change, then little by little, day by day, make the little adjustments that mean change. Let go of old habits and learn new ones. Watch what you are doing, ask God to help you make the changes you need to make, then *act* differently. Then you are practicing flexibility.

When you practice flexibility, you accept things you cannot change. You don't insist on having your own way all the time. You don't try to control other people. You know you can only control yourself. When you are flexible, you enjoy surprises.

What would flexibility look like if . . .

- You keep making the same mistake over and over?

- You decide you want to change one of your habits?

- Your family had something fun planned and it had to be cancelled at the last minute?

- You notice that some of your friends are avoiding you?

- The way you are doing a job isn't working very well?

Signs of Success

Congratulations! You are practicing flexibility when you . . .

- Are willing to change bad habits

- Ask the Creator for help

- Try imaginative new ways of doing things

- Don't insist on always getting your own way

- Can adjust when something unexpected happens

- Go with the flow. Trust the unexpected.

Keep trying! You need more practice when you . . .

- Believe that you have no room for improvement

- Are never willing to change your habits

- Believe that difficulties come only to punish you

- Always do things the same old way

- Insist on getting your own way

- Get really upset when unexpected things happen

- Don't like surprises

❈ *AFFIRMATION* ❈

I am flexible. I am willing to change myself for the better. I am open to new ways to do things. When trouble comes, I ask my Creator to help me learn from it. I welcome surprises.

❧ FORGIVENESS ❧

"To those who do wrong out of ignorance, then repent and correct themselves, your Lord is indeed forgiving and kind."
—AL-QUR'AN 16:19

What Is Forgiveness?

Everyone makes mistakes. Being forgiving is overlooking the mistakes others make and loving them just as much as before. Forgiving does not mean that all of a sudden you do not feel hurt or that the wrong choice someone made was right. It means that you find it in your heart to give the person another chance.

It means that in spite of how wrong they were or how much they hurt you, you can overlook what they did and not hold it against them. Forgiveness means you don't punish people for what they have done even if they deserve it.

You can even forgive yourself. You sometimes do things that you are sorry for and wish you hadn't done. Forgiving yourself means to stop punishing yourself or feeling hopeless because you did something wrong. It is moving ahead, ready to do things differently, with compassion for yourself and faith that you can change.

Why Practice Forgiveness?

The Creator gave us the power of free choice. This means it is up to us to do good or bad, right or wrong. For many, many reasons people sometimes choose to do wrong or hurtful things. Everyone does at one time or another.

Sometimes it is a little thing, such as not doing something we promised to do. Sometimes it is a bigger thing, like lying or taking something which doesn't belong to us. When someone who is hurt or disappointed forgives us, we get another chance. We can try again to do what's right.

Forgiveness is very important. If you do something you are sorry for and you forgive yourself, then you can learn from your mistakes. People who have trouble forgiving themselves often find it difficult to forgive others too.

If someone is not forgiving, others feel worried around that person. People who don't practice forgiveness judge and criticize others instead of giving them a chance to improve.

Forgiveness is the best way to encourage yourself and others to be better, to try harder, and to make changes.

How Do You Practice It?

You can practice forgiveness by first admitting the mistake that you or someone else has made. Facing the truth about what happened takes courage. You may feel sad and angry. Let your feelings come and then let them go, like leaves passing by in a stream.

When you are forgiving, you don't punish someone by taking revenge or holding a grudge. You don't punish yourself by calling yourself bad names.

Look at what happened, honor your feelings, think, and then decide what needs to change to make things right. God is always ready to forgive a mistake when someone is really sorry. You can too.

The hardest things to forgive in yourself are the things which you do over and over, habits you feel you cannot control. To truly forgive yourself takes action. Replacing old habits with new ones is one of the best ways to forgive yourself. If someone else does something hurtful to you over and over without being sorry, forgiving them won't help. You need to stop giving them the chance to hurt you.

When you make a mistake, ask the Creator to bless it and give you the courage to change. Forgiveness allows you to learn from mistakes. Sometimes they are your best teachers.

What would forgiveness look like if . . .

- Your friend accidentally broke your favorite toy?

- Your mother is late picking you up from school?

- You did something you feel is very bad?

- Your brother repeatedly takes something of yours without asking?

- Someone lost her temper with you and later apologized?

Signs of Success

Congratulations! You are practicing forgiveness when you . . .

- Remember that everyone makes mistakes

- Take responsibility for your mistakes

- Share your feelings without taking revenge

- Stop giving uncaring people the chance to hurt you

- Correct your mistakes instead of punishing yourself with guilt

- Accept God's forgiveness

Keep trying! You need more practice when you . . .

- Are afraid to look at your mistakes

- Judge and criticize others or yourself

- Take revenge or hold a grudge

- Allow careless people to keep hurting you

- Feel hopeless and helpless over bad habits

- Keep making the same mistakes without learning

⊰ *AFFIRMATION* ⊱

I am forgiving of myself and others. I learn from my mistakes. I have the power to keep changing for the better.

❧ FRIENDLINESS ❧

"*A friend is devoted at all times.*"
—PROVERBS 17:17

What Is Friendliness?

Friendliness is taking an interest in other people, being warm and courteous. When you are friendly, you happily share the things you have. You share your time, your ideas, and your feelings. You share yourself.

Friendliness is going out of your way to make others feel welcome or to make a stranger feel at home. Friendliness is sharing the good times and the bad times together.

Friendliness is caring without being asked to care. Friendliness is the best cure for loneliness.

❧ ❧ ❧

Why Practice Friendliness?

When people practice friendliness, it gives strangers a welcome feeling. Being friendly keeps you and others from feeling too lonely. When something good happens to you, or something bad, it feels good to share those feelings with someone else. To do that requires a friend.

When we have a friend, we can still be alone if we want. Or we can be with someone who loves us and cares about us. Our friends can do things with us and share their thoughts and ideas. When we make it easy for others to be friends with us, we are being friendly. Friendliness means we do not have to be alone unless we want to be.

Friendships don't just happen—they are made by people who are willing to be themselves with each other. Without friendliness we would find ourselves alone, without friends. Unless we are friendly, people believe we don't like them or care about them.

Many people are shy and need a very friendly person to go out of their way before they feel comfortable. Friendliness attracts people and allows them to get to know you and you to know them. Without friendliness people keep to themselves and have no one to feel close to or to share with.

How Do You Practice It?

Friendliness starts with liking yourself. If you do not feel good about yourself or believe you have things to share, you will stay away from others.

You can be friendly just by walking down the hall at school, looking into people's faces, and smiling at them. They will probably smile back.

Pick someone that you would like to get to know. Smile and greet that person. Ask her something about herself and listen to what she has to say.

Do something together. Share what you have with her (including your other friends). Invite her into your home. Invite others along if you feel like it.

Next time you see a friend, show him you are happy to see him. Ask him what has happened to him since you were together, and then tell him what's new for you.

When a friend is sad, don't always try to cheer him up right away. He might need to be sad for a while. Sit with him and ask him to tell you what he is sad about.

What would friendliness look like if . . .

- You see a child who has just moved into your neighborhood?

- You wish you could make friends with a popular student in school?

- Your parents invite a family over to dinner whom you have never met?

- One of your friends looks like she has been crying?

Signs of Success

Congratulations! You are practicing friendliness when you . . .

- Like yourself and realize you have a lot to offer

- Smile and greet people with courtesy

- Have the courage to introduce yourself

- Show an interest in others

- Ask people about themselves

- Show caring when a friend needs you

Keep trying! You need more practice when you . . .

- Do not like yourself and think no one else would like you either

- Keep your thoughts, feelings, and ideas to yourself

- Avoid people you don't know

- Do everything by yourself

- Do not share with others

- Don't ask others about themselves or don't listen when they talk

❧ *AFFIRMATION* ❧

I am friendly. Today I will smile and say hello to people. I will share myself and show an interest in others. I like myself, and I know I can make new friends.

❧ GENEROSITY ❦

"The gift which is given without thought of recompense, in the belief that it ought to be made, in a fit place, at an opportune time, and to a deserving person—such a gift is pure." —BHAGAVAD-GITA 17:20

What Is Generosity?

Generosity is giving and sharing. It is giving freely because you want to, not with the idea of receiving attention, a reward, or a gift in return. Giving freely also means you give without a concern for what someone does with your gift.

Generosity is a quality of the spirit. It is an awareness that there is plenty for everyone. It is seeing an opportunity to share what you have and then giving just for the joy of giving. It is one of the best ways to show love.

🌱 🌱 🌱

Why Practice Generosity?

Without generosity the world would be a sad place. People who need help would feel like beggars—without pride or dignity. In a world without generosity, every gift would have a string attached. Every gift would come with conditions that would enable the giver to gain something and to manipulate things for his own advantage. That is not giving.

When people do give freely, especially when there is some sacrifice involved, this is an important way to exercise their spirituality. Giving freely and fully is contagious. When one person is generous, it touches other people's hearts and then they want to be generous too. It just keeps going. Then everyone has more of what they need.

How Do You Practice It?

Generosity begins by recognizing some person or group that deserves your help. It could be your family. Then think of some way to help or something to give.

Look for things to share that mean something to you. You can share your time, knowledge, things, or money. Look for a way to give what you can—a way that gives others the feeling that they deserve what you are giving.

Don't look for anything in return. Don't look at how your gift is used—just give it freely and let it go. You'll feel good because you have given generously!

What would generosity look like if . . .

- A friend comes over to play the day after your birthday and you have a new toy?

- A friend who has broken your toys before wants to play with your favorite one?

- Your father is cooking dinner and needs someone to set the table, and you're watching your favorite TV show?

- A child in your class has forgotten her lunch and doesn't have any money?

- Someone's birthday is coming up and you wonder what to get him?

Signs of Success

Congratulations! You are practicing generosity when you . . .

- Are thoughtful about the needs of others

- Notice when someone needs help

- Give freely without hope of reward

- Give fully without holding back

- Are willing to make sacrifices for others

- Use wisdom about sharing treasured belongings

Keep trying! You need more practice when you . . .

- Cannot find anyone who deserves your help

- Keep giving to someone who abuses your help

- Give only things that do not matter to you

- Expect something in return for sharing

- Hold on to the gift after it is given with conditions about how it should be used

- Keep reminding people that you gave

❧ *AFFIRMATION* ❧

I am generous. I look for opportunities to give and to share. There is plenty of time for thoughtfulness. I give freely, fully, and joyfully.

❧ GENTLENESS ❧

> *"Love and affinity are the fruits of a gentle disposition, a pure nature and praiseworthy character."*
> —SELECTED WRITINGS OF ABDU'L-BAHA

What Is Gentleness?

Gentleness is acting and speaking in a way which is considerate and kind to others. It is using self-control in order not to hurt or offend anyone. Being gentle means to be very careful. You can be gentle with people and animals in the way you touch them and the way you speak to them. Being gentle with things means to be careful so that they will not break or be hurt in any way.

Gentleness is moving wisely, touching softly, holding carefully, speaking quietly, and thinking kindly.

🌱 🌱 🌱

Why Practice Gentleness?

People are very sensitive creatures. Many things are delicate and fragile, but feelings are the most fragile of all. When people are gentle with each other, feelings are protected and no one is hurt. When you handle things gently and carefully, they are less likely to be broken. When you think gentle thoughts, it makes the world a gentler place.

Without gentleness things are broken and feelings are hurt. Even if you do not mean to do it, you could play too roughly or say things that you will be sorry for. To be gentle, you have to think about being gentle. Otherwise, it is easy to become too rough. People who are too rough scare and hurt other people.

How Do You Practice It?

You practice gentleness by first "going inside" and deciding that you do not want to hurt or offend anyone or anything. Then you learn to control yourself, your body, your mind, and your voice. You try hard to be careful (full of care). You notice what your body, hands, and legs are doing and make an effort to move carefully.

When you play with someone, you make sure you are not hurting them. When you play with a toy, you treat it carefully so that it will not break. When you say something, you say it in a way that does not hurt the listener's feelings.

When you feel mad or hurt, instead of blowing up and hurting someone else, you use your voice to talk things out peacefully. You control yourself so that you don't hurt other people even when you feel angry.

Concentrate your thoughts on love and kindness, and people will see the gentleness in your eyes.

What would gentleness look like if . . .

- You want to touch or hold a baby?

- You have something to tell your friend which you think might hurt his feelings?

- You are setting the table with your family's best dishes?

- You walk in from school and start to slam the door?

- Your pet has been hurt and needs to be carried into the house?

- You're wrestling too roughly with a friend?

Signs of Success

Congratulations! You are practicing gentleness when you . . .

- Make it safe for animals and people to be around you

- Touch carefully

- Speak with a soft voice

- Express feelings peacefully

- Take time out when you don't feel gentle

- Think gentle thoughts that make you smile inside

Keep trying! You need more practice when you . . .

- Forget to consider other people's feelings

- Speak loudly or harshly

- Use things carelessly

- Play roughly

- Break things often

- Let your angry thoughts lead to treating others harshly

❧ *AFFIRMATION* ❧

I am gentle. I think, speak, and act with gentleness. I show care for people and for everything I touch.

❧ Helpfulness ❧

"Do not refuse a kindness to anyone who asks it, if it is in your power to perform it."
—Proverbs 3:27

What Is Helpfulness?

Helpfulness is being of service to someone. When you are being helpful, you do useful things that make a difference. Helpfulness can be doing something that others cannot do for themselves, things they don't have the time to do, or just little things that make life easier.

Helpfulness is not always doing what other people want. This is just pleasing people. What people want may not be useful or good for them. Helpfulness is giving people what they need, not always what they want.

You can be helpful to yourself by being sure that you have what you need. You can do things to help your body, such as eating the right foods, getting enough rest and exercise, or wearing clothes that will keep you from getting too hot or cold.

There are times when you may feel helpless. That is a good time to ask for help from others.

You deserve it.

Why Practice Helpfulness?

People often need help to meet their needs or get things done. Many things take the efforts of more than one person. If people didn't practice helpfulness, there would be no cooperation.

We all need help at times, whether we are learning something new and we need someone to teach us, or we are doing a hard job and need someone else's strength or ideas. Sometimes we just need a friend to talk to.

When people practice helpfulness, they care for each other. They make each other's lives easier. They are willing to cooperate to get things done.

When people come together to help one another, great things can be accomplished.

How Do You Practice It?

You practice helpfulness by noticing what people need. Look for opportunities to do a service for friends or people in your family or even someone you don't know. When you are practicing helpfulness, you don't wait for people to ask you. You notice what they need and just do it.

If you cannot figure out what someone needs, ask them, "How can I help?" or "Is there any help you need today?"

People (including you) need all kinds of things. Sometimes they need physical help, such as carrying a package when they have too many, or setting the table, or cleaning the house. They also need hugs, understanding, and appreciation. Sometimes the best help in the world is a listening ear.

When people ask you for help, it's important to decide for yourself if what they ask is really good for them. If not, it's probably more helpful not to do it.

It's important to ask others for help when you need it. And remember, you can always ask God.

What would helpfulness look like if . . .

- A friend is carrying a whole pile of books?

- It's time for dinner and your mother could use help?

- You notice that a friend looks sad?

- Your best friend asks you if she can copy your homework?

- Your baby brother spilled his milk on the rug and your mom is in another room?

- An older person just slipped and fell?

Signs of Success

Congratulations! You are practicing helpfulness when you . . .

- Notice when someone needs help

- Do a service without being asked

- Give people what they need, not always what they want

- Listen to someone who needs to talk

- Care for your own needs

- Ask for help when you need it

Keep trying! You need more practice when you . . .

- Act without thinking about what others need

- Do whatever anyone asks even if it isn't good for them

- Ignore others when they ask for help

- Fail to offer others recognition, appreciation, or a listening ear

- Ignore your own needs

- Never ask for help, even from God

✠ *AFFIRMATION* ✠

I am helpful. I look for ways to be of service. I care for others and myself. I look for helpful ways to make a difference.

⊱ HONESTY ⊰

> "*Beautify your tongues, O people, with truthfulness, and adorn your souls with the ornament of honesty. Beware, O people, that ye deal not treacherously with anyone.*"
> —WRITINGS OF BAHA'U'LLAH

What Is Honesty?

Being honest is being sincere, open, trustworthy, and truthful. When people are honest, they can be relied on not to lie, cheat, or steal. If they tell you they like you, you know they really mean it, because they would not say anything just to get their way or to make an impression.

If someone seems friendly, honesty means they really are friendly, just because they want to be friends, not for any hidden reasons. With honesty you can trust things to be as they appear.

Honesty is telling the truth no matter what. It is being truthful even when admitting the truth could make someone disappointed. Honesty means not exaggerating something just to impress others.

Being honest means you don't make false promises. You do what you said you would do. Your actions match your words. This is also called integrity.

Why Practice Honesty?

When someone lies, cheats, or steals, people around him can't trust him. If someone makes up stories to cover up a mistake, it's hard to correct the mistake. Then he feels worse and worse about himself.

Have you ever heard of false advertising? That's when people try to sell something by lying about it or exaggerating. How would you like to spend money on something and then find out that it doesn't do what it is supposed to—like a toy that doesn't really work? Without honesty people would always have to be suspicious.

Sometimes people aren't honest with themselves. They try to pretend that something doesn't matter even when it really does—like hurting someone's feelings. When someone isn't honest with herself about something, she usually isn't honest with others.

Honesty keeps you from deceiving or fooling other people just to get what you want. Honesty helps you not to fool yourself either. When you are honest with yourself, you have a chance to correct your mistakes. When you are honest with others, they know they can believe you.

How Do You Practice It?

Match your actions and your words. Avoid deception—don't try to fool anyone and don't let them fool you.

Say what you mean and mean what you say. When you do something, give it your best effort, and then don't pretend you did more. Don't say or do things just to make a good impression. You don't need to make things up to look good—you're quite fine as you are, honest!

Only make promises that you can honestly keep. Be trustworthy in all your dealings, refusing to lie, cheat, or steal.

Use your imagination, but don't let it keep you from telling the truth.

Tell the truth, no matter what. If you make a mistake, admit it. It's the best way to fix things. Be honest with yourself, and you will always be able to be honest with others.

What would honesty look like if . . .

- You broke one of your mother's favorite things by accident and are afraid she will be angry?

- You find yourself exaggerating about how well you did in a sports game to impress your friends?

- Your sister asks you if a new dress looks good on her and you think it looks pretty bad?

- You say something cruel to someone when you're mad and then tell yourself he deserved it?

- You forgot to do an important homework assignment and the teacher asks you where it is?

- Some friends of yours try to convince you to steal some candy from a store?

Signs of Success

Congratulations! You are practicing honesty when you . . .

- Say what you mean and mean what you say

- Make promises you can keep

- Admit your mistakes

- Tell the truth tactfully

- Refuse to cheat, steal, or lie

- Are true to yourself and do what you know is right

Keep trying! You need more practice when you . . .

- Lie, cheat, or steal

- Think you have to exaggerate to be important

- Cover it up when you make a mistake

- Promise to do things and then "forget"

- Fool yourself or permit others to fool you

- Hurt others by being honest without tact or kindness

❧ *AFFIRMATION* ❦

I am honest. I have integrity. I tell the truth, kindly and tactfully. I have no need to impress others or follow the crowd. I do what I know is right.

❧ ❈ HONOR ❈ ❧

"Supreme honor and real happiness lie in self-respect, in high resolves and noble purposes, in integrity and moral quality, in immaculacy of mind." —ABD'UL-BAHA

What Is Honor?

Being honorable is living with a sense of respect for what you believe is right. It is living by the virtues, living up to the gifts that the Creator placed within you. When you are honorable, you are worthy of the respect of others. You set a good example.

God created each one of us for a place of honor. Many people give up that place by continually making bad choices.

When you are being honorable, you don't feel ashamed of who you are or what you are doing. You are proud of the choices you are making.

People of honor distinguish themselves by doing what is right, regardless of what others are doing. Honor is a path of integrity.

🌱 🌱 🌱

Why Practice Honor?

Without honor people act disrespectfully and do things which make them and others feel ashamed. When they do something wrong, they don't try to correct it but just keep doing it over and over. Without honor they don't care about the virtues. They do just what they want without thinking of whether it is right or wrong. Other people don't respect them or want to be around them.

When someone is being honorable, other people know they can be trusted to do their best and try their hardest. Their word of honor means they will do exactly what they promised. People respect and rely on someone who is honorable.

How Do You Practice It?

When you act with honor, you do the right thing. You honor your agreements. When you say you will do something, no one has to remind or nag you. You honor your parents, teachers, and elders by speaking respectfully to them. You honor God by being your best self. You honor yourself at the same time.

When you want to be honorable, it helps to realize that God made you noble, capable of practicing all the virtues. Staying noble is up to you. When you are being honorable, you respect yourself. You make efforts to practice all of the virtues you have within you.

When you act with honor, you set a good example for others to follow, not because you are looking for admiration but just because it is the right thing to do.

What would honor look like if . . .

- Your friend told you a secret?

- You are mad at your mother when she asks you to do something?

- Someone tries to get you to steal some candy from a store?

- You find some money in the school hallway?

- Everyone is teasing a child in the playground?

- You promised to practice the piano while your parents were out?

Signs of Success

Congratulations! You are being honorable when you . . .

- Believe you were created noble

- Keep your agreements

- Speak respectfully to others

- Do what you believe is right no matter what

- Set a good example for others

- Avoid doing things which make you feel ashamed

Keep trying! You need more practice when you . . .

- Think you are not worthy of respect

- Don't honor your agreements

- Speak disrespectfully

- Do something wrong and hope you won't get caught

- Feel ashamed without doing something about it

- Give up on yourself

⇥ AFFIRMATION ⇤

I am honorable. I keep my agreements and treat others with respect. I live by the virtues. I care about doing the right thing.

❧ HUMILITY ❧

"So he sat down, and called the Twelve, and said to them, 'If anyone wants to be first, he must make himself last of all and servant of all.' " —MARK 9:33

What Is Humility?

When you are humble, you don't consider yourself more important than other people. You are happy to serve others and think other people's needs are important. When you are humble, you don't criticize others. You don't criticize or shame yourself either. Humility helps you to understand that life is for learning and to be aware that no matter how much you know, there is always more. It means that you don't expect to be perfect. When you make a mistake, you are willing to learn from it. When you need help, you are not too proud to ask for it.

Humility is doing your best without attracting too much attention to yourself. It is giving what you have to give, not to impress others, but just for the sake of giving.

❧ ❧ ❧

Why Practice Humility?

Humility is important because it keeps you focused on your own growth rather than the faults of others. If you worry about impressing others, they will start to tell you what they want you to be and you will lose part of yourself.

Humility helps you learn from mistakes instead of being ashamed of them. Humility helps you treat others as equals, different yet equal. Humility lets you learn from others.

It keeps you free from prejudice and from judging others.

How Do You Practice It?

To practice humility, don't pay a lot of attention to what others say about you, good or bad. Don't waste your energy trying to impress others. Just be yourself and do your best.

Humility helps you to realize everyone is a human being—each one different but still a person. You don't waste time trying to figure out who is more important, comparing yourself to others. Instead of competing, you strive to perfect your own gifts. When you do wonderful things, humility reminds you to be thankful instead of boastful.

When you are humble, you aren't afraid to ask for help when you need it. Everyone needs help sometimes.

When you are humble, you don't worry over your mistakes. Instead you are eager to learn from them. You pay attention to what you have to learn rather than what you have already done. You keep on growing all of your life. You don't ever act as if you are finished.

What would humility look like if . . .

- You notice that you can run much faster than your friend?

- You notice that your friend usually gets better marks in school than you do?

- You make a big mistake and also hurt someone's feelings?

- Your brother or sister does a chore and you think they should have done a better job?

- What is one of the "best" mistakes you ever made—one that taught you the most?

Signs of Success

Congratulations! You are practicing humility when you . . .

- Realize that everyone is a human being—each one different but still a person

- Respect what each person contributes

- Learn from your mistakes

- Ask for help when you need it

- Are doing your best just to do it, not to impress anyone

- Are thankful instead of boastful

Keep trying! You need more practice when you . . .

- Believe that some people are born better than others

- Judge yourself or others

- Compete and compare

- Feel you are better or worse than others

- Do things to impress others

- Boast about your accomplishments

❧ AFFIRMATION ❧

I am humble. I learn from my mistakes. I do not judge others or myself. I value my ability to keep growing.

❧ IDEALISM ❧

> *"Let your acts be a guide unto all mankind, for the professions of most men, be they high or low, differ from their conduct. It is through your deeds that ye can distinguish yourselves from others. Through them the brightness of your light can be shed upon the whole earth."*
>
> —WRITINGS OF BAHA'U'LLAH

What Is Idealism?

A person with "high ideals" is someone who really cares about what is right and meaningful in life. When you practice idealism, you have beliefs that mean something to you and you follow them. You don't just accept things the way they are.

Being an idealist means believing in making the world a better place. You believe it so much that you are willing to work really hard to make it happen. You don't ignore problems when you see them, such as people going hungry or someone being treated unjustly. You want to make a difference.

Idealists dare to have big dreams and then act as if they are possible. They can imagine something and then do it.

Idealism does not mean that you are an idle dreamer. Idle dreamers just wish that things were better. Idealists do something to make things better.

Why Practice Idealism?

When people don't have ideals, they just live as if nothing matters very much. They have no dreams of what is possible. They settle for whatever happens.

People without ideals don't strive to improve the conditions in the world. Without idealism things would stay just as they are. No one would have a vision of how things could be better or even what is possible. The best they would hope for is that things wouldn't get worse. No one would be trying to improve; no one would be growing or developing. Unless people have ideals, when bad things happen, they would just let them. People would get more and more discouraged.

When you practice idealism, you know that tomorrow will be better than today. You know what is possible and you act to make it happen.

How Do You Practice It?

Idealism begins by picturing what you would ideally like to see happen. It is visualizing wonderful possibilities. It could be a vision of what you will be like when you grow up. Then you decide to make it happen. You look at where you are and where you want to go and make a plan to get there. People who accomplish great things have all started with an ideal.

You might want to picture having an ideal friend. That would be someone who would be just perfect for you to enjoy and spend time with. A good way to attract the ideal in your life is to do something to make it real. You could strive each day to *be* the ideal friend. And it would probably work.

There are usually people around to tell you that your dream is impossible. When you are practicing idealism, you make a plan and then stick with it no matter what. You can ask God to guide you too.

Make sure that your words and your actions match. Don't say you believe in peace, for example, and then go around bashing people. Practicing the virtues is a great way to make the ideal real in your life.

What would idealism look like if . . .

- You would like to see your school free of prejudice?

- People tell you that your dream is impossible?

- You want to make the ideal gift for your mother?

- You feel somewhat hopeless about achieving a goal?

- You have a dream of becoming a great musician?

Signs of Success

Congratulations! You are practicing idealism when you . . .

- Really care about what you value in life

- Dare to have big dreams

- Have a vision of what is possible

- Have a plan to make your ideals real

- Do something to make a difference

- Ask God for help and guidance

Keep trying! You need more practice when you . . .

- Just settle for the way things are

- Don't care much about anything

- Think having dreams and ideals is silly

- Give up easily on what you believe

- Don't have any visions of what you want to see in your life and in the world

- Go along with other people's ideas of what matters

❧ *AFFIRMATION* ❧

I am practicing my ideals. My actions match my words. I believe in my dreams and have faith that with God's help, anything is possible.

✽ JOYFULNESS ✽

> "*Joy gives us wings! In times of joy our strength is more vital, our intellect keener, and our understanding less clouded. We seem better able to cope with the world and to find our sphere of influence.*"
>
> —ABDU'L-BAHA, PARIS TALKS

What Is Joyfulness?

Joyfulness is being filled with happiness, peace, love, and a sense of well-being. Joy is inside us all. It comes from a sense of being loved. It comes from an appreciation for the gift of life. It comes when we are doing what we know is right. Joy is related to fun but is not exactly the same thing. Fun comes from what is happening outside—having a good time. Joy comes from what is happening inside.

Joyfulness is always there regardless of what is happening on the outside. You can invest this inner joy in anything you do. You can enjoy doing your chores or your homework, even a job that's boring or unpleasant. If you look inside and find your joy, you can make it a joyful job.

Joy is the inner sense that can carry us through hard times, even when we are feeling very sad.

Why Practice Joyfulness?

Without inner joy all our feelings are determined by what is happening to us. When things are going well on the outside, we feel good. When things are going wrong on the outside, we feel bad. Up and down, up and down. Without an inner sense of joy we feel bounced around by the pain and pleasure of whatever is happening to us. Without joyfulness, when the fun stops, our happiness stops. Without joyfulness sadness gets deeper and deeper.

If we are joyful, things still happen to us, some good and some bad. If we are joyful, down deep we stay calm and serene. We continue to feel loved and safe. When good things happen, we are glad and the happy feelings last longer. When we are hurt, we naturally feel sad. When we draw on the inner strength of joyfulness, sadness does not keep getting deeper and deeper. It just comes and goes.

How Do You Practice It?

Joyfulness comes from your spirit—you find it inside. You are aware that life is a gift.

Whatever you are doing, do it with a joyful heart. When good things happen to you, enjoy them fully. When sad things happen, let the sadness come. Then let it go. Find the gifts in what is happening—is this a way to become stronger? Something new to learn?

Joyfulness comes when you have a good laugh. Humor is a wonderful source of joy.

Let yourself feel your inner peace and joy even when things are tough. Hard times pass. Remember you are always loved. You have been since before you were born.

What would joyfulness look like if . . .

- Your parents asked you to clean out the garage?

- A friend you like a lot moves away?

- You have a tough homework assignment?

- You spend some time meditating about your life?

- You feel sad and down?

Signs of Success

Congratulations! You are practicing joyfulness when you . . .

- Look inside for your inner happiness

- Believe that God created you and loves you always

- Enjoy whatever it is that you are doing

- Appreciate some gift in your life

- Appreciate some gift in yourself

- Feel an inner peace even when things are tough

- Remember to laugh

Keep trying! You need more practice when you . . .

- Always look outside yourself for your fun and happiness

- Enjoy life only when things are going well

- Forget to appreciate the gifts in your life

- Feel so sad when bad things happen that you cannot learn from them at all

- Often get stuck in negative feelings

- Keep a frown on your face

❧ *AFFIRMATION* ❧

I am thankful for the joy I feel inside. I enjoy my work and my play. I appreciate the gifts this day holds for me.

❧ JUSTICE ❧

"He who possesses character and discrimination, who is just, speaks the truth, and does what is his own business, him the world will hold dear." —DHAMMAPADA 217

What Is Justice?

Practicing justice is being fair in everything you do. It is seeing with your own eyes and not judging something or someone by what other people tell you.

Justice means that people receive what they deserve. Everyone gets his fair share. It is just for people to receive a consequence or punishment when they do something wrong, so they will remember to do things differently next time. It is also just for people to be recognized when they are doing something right or making an improvement.

Being just is standing up for your rights and the rights of other people. If someone is taking advantage of you, it is not just to allow them to continue doing it. If someone is hurting you, it is just to stop them. It is never just for strong people to hurt weaker people. Justice means that every person's rights are protected.

When you practice being just, you treat each person as an individual. You don't judge people or put them in categories. You just see them one by one.

Why Practice Justice?

Without justice people who hurt or take advantage of others get away with it and keep on doing it. Without justice the world can be a cruel and dangerous place. People are judged or treated differently because of their sex, race, or religion. Innocent people, like young children, suffer for no reason. People with wealth and power get away with things that poor people cannot. We need justice in order to protect the rights of everyone.

When justice is practiced, people can expect to receive what they deserve. If they work to earn money, they receive it.

If they do something well, they are recognized and rewarded for it. If they are accused of something, they have a chance to say what really happened and to be heard fairly.

When people are being just, they don't separate themselves from other human beings because they look or sound different or come from a different culture. Everyone has a fair chance to be seen for who they are.

When there is justice, everyone receives a fair share.

How Do You Practice It?

Being just is investigating the truth for yourself, accepting what others say only as their opinion. You see the facts with your own eyes and ears. You think for yourself.

When you are just, you act without prejudice by seeing each person as an individual. You don't decide things about them because of their race, color, nationality, religion, or sex, whether they are fat or thin, rich or poor.

When you are just, you admit your own mistakes and accept the consequences. You share with others—so everyone has a fair share.

When you are practicing justice, you don't gossip or find fault behind someone's back. It wouldn't be fair, because they aren't there to tell their side of things. If you have a problem with someone, you go directly to that person and work things out.

When you are being just, you stand up for yourself and for others. You don't accept it when someone acts like a bully, cheats, or lies. Being a champion for justice takes courage. Sometimes when you stand for justice, you stand alone.

What would being just look like if . . .

- You are with a group and they start to gossip?

- Everyone is teasing a child who looks different?

- Someone makes a remark to you about people of a different race?

- An older child starts to get rough with you?

- Something in your room is missing and you think your brother took it?

- You are cutting the cake at your birthday party?

Signs of Success

Congratulations! You are practicing justice when you . . .

- Think for yourself

- Look for the truth by investigating things for yourself

- Avoid gossip and backbiting

- Refuse to pre-judge. See people as individuals

- Own up to your mistakes and accept the consequences

- Share fairly with others

- Stand up for people's rights, including your own

Keep trying! You need more practice when you . . .

- Follow what others think or believe

- Gossip or backbite instead of working out a problem with someone directly

- Base your beliefs about people on prejudice

- Avoid getting involved if someone is being abused

- Try to get away with things you know are wrong

- Treat people differently based on how they look or what they have

❧ *AFFIRMATION* ❧

I act with justice. I investigate the truth for myself and form my own opinions. I do not gossip or backbite. I stand up for the rights of others and myself.

❧ KINDNESS ❧

*"**B**e ye sincerely kind, not in appearance only. Let each one of God's loved ones center his attention on this: to be the Lord's mercy to man; to be the Lord's grace. Let him do some good to every person whose path he crosseth, and be of some benefit to him."*

—SELECTIONS FROM THE
WRITINGS OF ABDU'L-BAHA

What Is Kindness?

Kindness is being concerned about the welfare of others. Kindness is showing you care about anyone or anything that crosses your path, knowing that everything is a part of God's creation. You can be kind to people, to animals, and to the environment. Kindness means to care for others and the earth as much as or more than you care about yourself.

Kindness is shown in small gestures that brighten people's lives, times you care for an animal, daily ways you show concern for the earth. Kindness is showing love to someone who is sad or needs your help.

🌱 🌱 🌱

Why Practice Kindness?

Without kindness no one would listen when people or animals need help. Everyone would be looking out for herself. The world is lonely without kindness. When someone reaches out to another in an act of kindness, it helps them both. Everything in the world God created is connected. If we are unkind to any part of it, it affects us as well.

People's selfishness and lack of kindness to the earth has caused damage to the air, the water, the land. This has brought suffering to people and animals too. Being kind allows us to feel the connectedness we have with all other things. Being kind makes things better for every one of us.

How Do You Practice It?

You practice kindness by noticing when someone or something needs care. You become sensitive to the world around you. Use your imagination to think of things that give others happiness—your parents, your friends, your teachers, your brothers and sisters, and even people you don't know very well. Find out what habits harm or help the environment and choose kinder ways.

When you are tempted to be cruel, to criticize or tease, you decide not to do it (even with your own brothers and sisters!). You accept people who are different or handicapped instead of ignoring them or teasing them. When you are practicing kindness, you take really good care of your pets.

What would kindness look like if . . .

- A new child comes into your class and she looks lonely?

- You start teasing your brother and he is getting upset?

- Some kids you have been playing with start ridiculing a boy who has big ears?

- Your cat has gotten some burrs in her fur?

- Your mother seems tired lately?

Signs of Success

Congratulations! You are practicing kindness when you . . .

- Give tender attention to someone who is sad or needs help

- Do things that give others happiness

- Practice habits that help the earth (reduce, reuse, recycle)

- Resist the temptation to be cruel in your words or actions

- Accept people who are different

- Take good care of animals

- Remember your connection to all of creation

Keep trying! You need more practice when you . . .

- Always put yourself first

- Don't pay attention to the needs of others

- Don't think about how you can help the environment

- Tease and play tricks on others

- Ignore or ridicule someone who is different

- Hurt animals

- Neglect your pets

- Forget that you are part of God's creation and that all of it deserves to be cared for with kindness

❧ *AFFIRMATION* ❧

I am kind. I look for ways to help others. I show kindness to any person or animal I see. I do all I can to take care of the earth. I remember my connection to all creation.

❦ LOVE ❦

"Thou shalt not take vengeance, nor bear any grudge against the children of thy people, but thou shalt love thy neighbor as thyself." —LEVITICUS 19:18

What Is Love?

Love is caring for someone, wanting to be near them, and wanting to share with them. Love is the power of attraction. It is a special feeling that fills your heart. Loving people means treating them with special care and kindness because they mean so much to you.

You can show love in a smile, a pleasant way of speaking, a thoughtful act, or a hug.

Love is putting yourself in someone else's shoes and caring about what they feel. It is accepting them just as they are. You can even be loving to strangers, just by caring what happens to them, and sending loving thoughts.

Love is treating other people just as you would like them to treat you—with care and respect.

Why Practice Love?

Without love people would feel very lonely. When people don't feel that they matter to anyone, they become unhappy. Sometimes they act angry and treat others carelessly. They don't let others get close to them and have trouble sharing and trusting.

Everyone wants to be liked. Everyone likes to be loved. When you are being loving, you help others to feel important. When people know they are loved, they are nicer and kinder. Love is contagious. It keeps spreading. When you love God, you can feel God's love for you. When you love yourself, you have more love to give.

How Do You Practice It?

You practice being loving by allowing yourself to feel love. Sometimes it just comes. You could be watching a little bird, looking at your mother, or noticing a new person and wanting very much to make friends. Showing that you care is a way to be loving. You can do all kinds of thoughtful little things to show love.

Sharing is a way to be loving. You can share your belongings, your time, and yourself—your ideas, feelings, opinions, affection, and attention.

Love is showing compassion for other people and wishing for them what you wish for yourself. Think about how you would like them to treat you and then treat them the same way. Loving yourself makes this much easier. When you practice being loved, you are kind and forgiving to yourself and others.

You can show your love for God by talking with God in prayer and by being loving to all the people God created with love.

What would love look like if . . .

- You start to get upset with yourself about something you have done?

- You want to do something thoughtful when your father is sick?

- Another child is acting cranky?

- You notice a baby bird has fallen out of its nest?

- You love your teacher and feel like showing it?

Signs of Success

Congratulations! You are practicing love when you . . .

- Treat others as you would want them to treat you

- Say kind and loving things

- Do little things that give others happiness

- Share your things and yourself

- Show affection

- Express love for the Creator by caring for others

- Think loving thoughts

Keep trying! You need more practice when you . . .

- Feel bad about yourself—feel like you have nothing to give

- Avoid other people and do as little as possible for them

- Don't give any thought to what others need or feel

- Say or do mean, unkind things

- Don't show affection

- Can't forgive yourself or others

❧ *AFFIRMATION* ❧

I am a loving person. I show my love with thoughtful acts, kind words, and affection. I treat others as I want to be treated. I love God and all that God created, including myself.

❧ LOYALTY ❧

> *"Those who keep their minds fixed on me, who worship me always with unwavering faith and concentration; these are the very best."* —BHAGAVAD-GITA XII, 2

What Is Loyalty?

Loyalty is standing up for something you believe in, having unwavering faith. Loyalty is being faithful to your family, country, friends, or ideals.

It is standing by a person, country, or cause when the going gets tough as well as when things are good. When you are a loyal friend, even if someone disappoints or hurts you, you still hang in there with them.

When you practice loyalty, you don't change from day to day. You stay true to someone or something unless you have a reason to believe that your loyalty has been betrayed. Loyalty is based on commitments—ones you make and plan to keep forever.

When you practice loyalty, people know what you stand for. Your friends and family know that you will support them no matter what happens. When you are loyal in your commitment to others, they know that nothing can come between you.

Why Practice Loyalty?

Without loyalty people would change their commitments as often as they change their clothes. One day they stand for this, the next day they stand for that. You can't count on people who are not loyal because when the going gets tough, disloyal people go away. Those that counted on them for support are betrayed. Disloyal people promise that they will be there forever. The next day they are gone.

When you practice loyalty, people know they can count on you. People who are worthy of your loyalty can trust that they will never have to stand alone. When you practice loyalty, you build friendships that last forever.

How Do You Practice It?

You practice loyalty by making a commitment to a person, country, or ideal. You have to be very careful about choosing what you commit yourself to, because if you are loyal, you will stand behind that commitment for a long time. Be sure that a person, belief, or country continues to be worthy of your loyalty. If someone tries to use your loyalty for a bad purpose or breaks faith with you, you need to decide whether it feels right to you to go on being loyal.

Loyalty is being strong in what you believe or care about. It is safeguarding something or someone you believe in. When you are loyal, you support a person, a country, or a cause during good times and bad.

If you are loyal to your family, you stand up for your brother or sister when others are acting unjustly toward them. When you are loyal, you are worthy of trust.

What would loyalty look like if . . .

- One friend tries to get you to turn against another?

- A group invites you to join their club but doesn't want your friends around?

- Someone you like says that if you are a true friend, you will lie for him?

- You believe in your religion and other people make fun of it?

- Someone starts teasing your sister in front of you?

- A friend suggests you "borrow" from your mom's purse?

Signs of Success

Congratulations! You are practicing loyalty when you . . .

- Are supportive to people and ideas you believe in

- Are faithful through good times and bad

- Stick with your commitment unless you have a really good reason to change it

- Don't allow blind loyalty to lead you into trouble

- Don't let others come between you and someone or something you care about

- Protect what you are loyal to whenever it is threatened

Keep trying! You need more practice when you . . .

- Don't consider anyone or anything important enough to be committed

- Leave your friends whenever someone more interesting comes along

- Are a "fair-weather" friend. Leave relationships when they become difficult.

- Change your commitments whenever you feel like it

- Have blind loyalty to someone or something that does not deserve it

- Talk about someone behind her back

❧ *AFFIRMATION* ❧

I am loyal to the people I care about. I am a good friend through good times and bad. I am loyal to what I know is right. I do not allow friendship to lead me into trouble.

❧ MERCY ❧

"Blessed are those who show mercy; mercy shall be shown to them." —MATTHEW 5:7

What Is Mercy?

Justice is giving people what they deserve. Mercy is giving people more than they deserve. Mercy is a quality of the heart. Being merciful means to treat others with compassion and forgiveness. When you are being merciful, you are willing to forgive when you have been hurt.

Being merciful is being willing to start all over, to wipe the slate clean of all mistakes or hurts and give people another chance. God is very merciful to us—by giving us lots of blessings and lots of chances to keep learning from our mistakes.

Mercy means you feel for someone who is suffering and do something to help them. A mercy is a blessing. When you practice mercy, you are giving others the gift of your tenderness.

🌱 🌱 🌱

Why Practice Mercy?

Without mercy the world would be a harsh and cruel place. We all make mistakes. Without mercy we would be punished for every mistake, even if it was an accident and we didn't mean to do it. Without mercy we would have to earn every good thing that came to us. People would stop before doing something kind and loving and say, "Hmmm. Do you really deserve this?" Without mercy, when we hurt someone, we would never get a second chance.

When we practice mercy, we give each other another chance when we make a mistake or do something hurtful. We forgive each other, and the relationship is not damaged forever.

When we are merciful with each other, it comes right back. Instead of showing love or kindness only when someone has earned it, we just go ahead and love each other. Mercy brings a gentleness which makes us feel safe with one another.

How Do You Practice It?

To practice mercy, it helps to put yourself in someone else's shoes. Especially when they do something that hurts or bothers you, you can think about how it feels when you do something wrong and how you wish someone else would treat you. Being kind and forgiving when someone has made a mistake, especially if they didn't mean to, is a good way to practice being merciful.

When you want to be merciful and someone has done something wrong, first you need to decide what would be the just way to deal with it. Then you decide if it would be better (and more merciful) for them to suffer the consequence of their actions or to get another chance. Being merciful when someone really needs justice in order to learn doesn't really help them.

You can be merciful to people you don't even know when your heart is touched by their suffering and you do what you can to help.

What would mercy look like if . . .

- Your friend accidentally broke one of your best toys?

- Someone stepped on your toe when you were standing in line?

- You hear about some children who don't have enough to eat?

- One of your parents is very cranky lately?

- Another child tries to trip you for the tenth time?

- A friend at school forgot his lunch?

Signs of Success

Congratulations! You are practicing mercy when you . . .

- Know what people deserve and choose to give them more than they have earned

- Give people another chance when they make a mistake

- Overlook hurtful things people do

- Put yourself in other people's shoes

- Let your heart be touched by people who are troubled and do something to help

Keep trying! You need more practice when you . . .

- Do not understand the difference between justice and mercy

- Hold grudges and always punish people who deserve it

- Get even for every little thing

- Make people do something to earn everything they receive from you

- Blame people for being poor or having problems

- Fail to act with justice when someone repeatedly and deliberately is hurtful to you

❧ AFFIRMATION ❧

I show mercy to others. I put myself in their shoes and do what I can to be helpful. I give others another chance when they make a mistake. I listen to my heart.

❧ MODERATION ❦

"One who lives without looking for pleasures, his senses well controlled, moderate in his food, faithful and strong, . . . the temptor will certainly not overthrow, any more than the wind throws down a rock mountain."
—DHAMMAPADA 8

What Is Moderation?

Moderation is creating balance in your life. It means you don't do the same thing all the time. Doing school work all the time or playing all the time is not being moderate. Being moderate is studying enough and playing enough, working enough and resting enough. Moderation is stopping before you go overboard. It is using self-discipline to keep from overdoing.

Too little of something is as immoderate as too much. People who talk too much can be disruptive. People who don't talk much at all get ignored, and when there is a discussion, their special way of thinking about things is missing.

Moderation is what keeps us from being blown about in the wind of our desires.

🌱 🌱 🌱

Why Practice Moderation?

Without moderation people go to one extreme or another. Either they ask for too much and then waste it, or deny themselves and don't have what they need to grow healthy in body and spirit. Without moderation people can get swept away and damage themselves by things like drugs or alcohol.

Without moderation people can become greedy. Other people get mad when they take too much food, talk too much, hang around too much, or sleep too much. Without moderation people don't do enough. Other people feel hurt when they don't do their share of the work, won't talk, or don't want to play because they are too tired.

Without moderation we can forget what enough means and overdo. We can start getting addicted to things and want more and more. Even things you like can hurt you if you have too much—like too much television or too much chocolate. When we have too much of something, we can find ourselves out of control.

Moderation keeps us from being controlled by our desires. When we practice moderation, we create a sense of balance in our lives. With moderation we are much more likely to get what we actually need. When we practice moderation, other people benefit too.

How Do You Practice It?

You practice moderation by getting what you need—not too much and not too little. You don't take more or less than you need of food, exercise, playtime, or sleep.

Learning your own limits is the first step of practicing moderation. What is too much or too little for you? People are different. For some people eight hours of sleep is too much; for some it is too little.

Then you practice wisdom and self-discipline to be sure that you get what you need. If you need nine hours of sleep to be healthy, make sure that you get those nine hours. Self-discipline helps you to stop yourself before things go too far. If eating six helpings of chocolate cake is past your limit, then maybe two would be kinder to your stomach (not to mention other cake eaters!).

Watch yourself to see if you are getting addicted to anything. It could be TV or computer games, or a food, or a person. Ask yourself what balance you need so that having more and more of something doesn't start to rule your life. When you practice moderation, you are content to have what you need.

What would moderation look like if . . .

- You like someone so much that you start to call her up and hang around her house every single day?

- You open the cookie jar and find your favorite cookies?

- You stay up late to read or play but then feel sleepy in the morning?

- You find you are spending all your free time playing a video game and don't see your friends anymore?

- You spend your whole allowance on chocolate bars and then it's gone?

Signs of Success

Congratulations! You are practicing moderation when you . . .

- Know what you need and get enough—no more, no less

- Take care of your health by getting enough of what you need

- Are content with enough

- Use self-discipline to stop yourself from overdoing

- Have a balance in your life between work and play

- Know your own limits and set boundaries for yourself

Keep trying! You need more practice when you . . .

- Don't know what you need or how much

- Get addicted to food, things, or people—want more and more

- Ignore limits and rules

- Do without what you really need

- Get too greedy and don't share with others

❧ *AFFIRMATION* ❧

I am moderate. I am thankful and content to get what I need. Work and play are balanced in my life. I don't overdo or underdo but find what's just right for me.

❧ MODESTY ❧

> *"He has told you what is good and what the lord requires of you: only to do justice and to love virtue and to walk modestly with your God."*
> —MICAH 6:8

What Is Modesty?

Modesty is having a sense of self-respect. When you practice modesty you are not showy or boastful. Modesty comes when you have a sense of self-acceptance and quiet pride. Modesty is to value yourself and to have a sense of privacy about your body.

Modesty means having a sense of what is appropriate and inappropriate about showing your body as well as how you allow others to touch you. It is keeping the private parts of your body to yourself and not allowing others to touch you in ways that abuse your privacy. People who practice modesty wear clothing which is both attractive and respectful.

Modesty means to accept praise without getting conceited or puffed up with a feeling of superiority. You are grateful for your gifts, and you know that others have gifts too.

Why Practice Modesty?

Without modesty people do all kinds of things just to attract attention. They brag and boast. They even allow others to take advantage of them and use them in disrespectful ways. Without modesty people don't set boundaries about how they wish to be touched or not touched. They often feel used by others and don't know why.

Without modesty people sing their own praises, and their virtues get lost in the noise. Bragging puts people off, so immodest people can become quite lonely.

When people practice modesty, they don't need to tell others how great they are. They just let their actions and their virtues speak for them. They show self-respect and then others respect them too.

How Do You Practice It?

Modesty is an attitude. It begins by being comfortable with yourself. It is knowing that you have special gifts and that others do as well. Humility helps in the practice of modesty.

When you do something with others, you don't take all the credit. You don't brag or boast or show off. You accept praise without getting conceited. You share your excitement about something you have done without making it sound like the best thing that anyone ever did.

Modesty is practiced when you keep others from exploiting you. You are respectful of your body and your privacy, and you expect others to be too. If anyone touches you in a way which doesn't feel right, go and tell an adult you trust. Don't keep it a secret.

When you are modest, you don't try to attract too much attention to yourself. You dress in a moderate and respectful way.

What would modesty look like if . . .

- A friend tries to convince you to buy a flashy outfit because everyone else is wearing it?

- Someone starts to tease you and tickle your private parts?

- You played really well and your team won the game?

- Someone wants to kiss you and you don't want him to?

- You feel like bragging about something good you did?

Signs of Success

Congratulations! You are practicing modesty when you . . .

- Are comfortable being who you are

- Respect yourself

- Do not permit anyone to abuse your body

- Set boundaries about your right to privacy

- Dress in a way which feels right to you

- Share your victories without boasting

- Share the credit with others who deserve it

Keep trying! You need more practice when you . . .

- Need to attract attention to feel important

- Rely on words more than deeds

- Dress in a way which disrespects yourself or others

- Constantly let others know how great you are

- Allow anyone to use or abuse your body

- Take too much credit instead of sharing it with others who deserve it too

❧ *AFFIRMATION* ❧

I am modest. I have no need to brag or attract attention. I am worthy of attention just as I am.

❧ OBEDIENCE ❦

> *"Children, obey your parents; for it is only right that you should. 'Honor your father and your mother' is the first commandment to carry a promise with it: 'that it may be well with you and that you may live long on the earth.'"*
> —EPHESIANS 6:1–2

What Is Obedience?

The purpose of obedience is to guide you and protect you. You need to think for yourself, and to feel sure that when you are obeying someone, even in your own family, that doing so is for your own good and will not hurt you or others.

When you are obedient, you abide by the rules, even if you don't like them, or it takes a lot of self-discipline to do so. You obey the rules even when no one is watching. To be obedient is to be trustworthy.

❧ ❧ ❧

Why Practice Obedience?

Being obedient keeps you safe and happy. When people don't care about obedience, they do just what they want even when it hurts themselves or other people. If everyone drove as fast as they wanted, many more people would be hurt or killed. If you rode your bicycle on the wrong side of the road, you could easily have an accident. There are many dangers in the world. Without obedience it is easy to get hurt or lost.

When you obey people who care for and want to protect you, it brings freedom and safety. If you know where it is safe to play, you can feel free of worry about unnecessary dangers. The same is true for laws created to protect the community. When everyone obeys the law, we can trust each other.

When people in a family abide by the family rules and keep their agreements, such as who does the dishes Thursday night, or who cares for the pets, it keeps things running smoothly. When you obey your inner guidance, your life gains order and discipline. You can trust yourself.

How Do You Practice It?

Obedience begins by doing what you are asked to do—by your family, your teachers, your country, or your faith.

Obedience is playing by the rules. It keeps things fair. Use your willpower to follow the rules, even when you feel like breaking them or ignoring them. Take responsibility for keeping agreements rather than waiting to be reminded. Be faithful to what your parents, elders, and teachers ask of you even when no one is watching. Follow the laws of the land in which you live.

Be respectful of those in authority when they tell you what to do, even if you don't agree with or understand it. If you need to question a rule or decision, do it respectfully and then do what you know is truly right.

Obey your own inner authority, that place of truth within you which knows what is right. Have the courage to stand for what is true.

If you break a law and there are consequences to pay, have the courage to learn from your mistake. Face the consequences willingly. Then forgive yourself and get a fresh start.

Don't be afraid to try again.

What would obedience look like if . . .

- You want to join a friend across a busy street and feel like rushing over to her without using the crosswalk?

- You want to spend the night at a friend's home and your parents tell you that you can't? You think they are being unfair.

- You're visiting your grandparents for the summer, and they have different rules for bedtime, baths, and chores than you are used to at home?

- Someone in authority tries to get you to do something which you feel is wrong or hurtful?

Signs of Success

Congratulations! You are practicing obedience when you . . .

- Use your willpower to follow the rules, even when you feel like breaking or ignoring them

- Keep your agreements without having to be reminded

- Do what is right even when no one is watching

- Question authority respectfully

- Accept the consequences if you break a rule or law—then get a fresh start

- Listen to your own inner authority

Keep trying! You need more practice when you . . .

- Don't know what the rules are and don't care to learn them

- Resent the guidance of elders, teachers, or the laws of the land— just do whatever you want

- Ignore laws which keep you and others safe

- Question a decision or rule by whining, complaining, or getting mad

- Need people to tell you three or four times before doing anything

- Obey only if someone is watching

- Never question authority, even when it hurts you or others

❊ *AFFIRMATION* ❊

I am obedient. I listen respectfully to my elders. I have the courage to face a just consequence and make a new start. I listen to my inner truth and do what is right.

❧ ORDERLINESS ❧

"Thus saith the Lord: 'Set thy house in order.'"
—KINGS II 20:1

What Is Orderliness?

Orderliness is being neat and living with a sense of harmony. It is having a place for the things you use and keeping them there so that you can use them whenever you need to.

Orderliness means being organized. It is planning something so that it works, staying on track, and doing something step by step instead of going in circles. Being orderly makes it easier to accomplish things.

It is being neat and careful when you are doing something so that it will be done as cleanly and beautifully as possible.

When you set your house in order, it can mean that you keep your room neat and clean, or that you are correcting some problem or mistake. When you have done something you feel is wrong, you can put things right again by changing yourself for the better.

When you appreciate the order of God's creation, you can see the beauty and harmony of all living things.

Why Practice Orderliness?

Without order people would always be running around looking for things, or feeling lost and confused. When you don't have a place for your things, they can get lost too.

People who need to do things precisely and quickly need to be especially orderly. What would happen if doctors couldn't find their instruments during an operation, or firefighters didn't put their equipment away so it would be ready to go the moment the fire alarm rings?

When people don't behave in an orderly way, things get all mixed up. When people are being orderly, they do things without wasted energy or effort.

When you are orderly, you can take any problem and plan a solution. If you have made a big mistake, you can put it right. Even something that is very difficult can be dealt with if you take it step by step, day by day.

When you appreciate the order of God's creation, you see the beauty all around you and can reflect it in your own life. When you create order around you, it makes your soul feel peaceful.

How Do You Practice It?

One of the most important ways to practice being orderly is to decide how and where you want to keep the things you use, like your clothes and toys, and put them where they belong when you are finished using them. You pick things up and put them away. You keep things that belong together in the same place. That way you always know where they are and don't have to waste energy finding them.

If you want to do something efficiently, first make a plan and then follow it. Don't let yourself get distracted. When something is difficult, divide it into pieces and do them one at a time.

Create an orderly, peaceful space where you live. It may mean making a painting with your favorite color and putting it up on the wall, or arranging your bed in a certain way that you like, or keeping your things on shelves. Keep your home as clean and orderly as you can.

Keeping your life in order brings a feeling of peace and freedom.

What would orderliness look like if . . .

- You look at your room and see a big mess?

- You finish playing with a game that has lots of pieces?

- You find it really hard to deal with some problem?

- You're running around the schoolyard with your friends and you hear the bell ring?

- You're on a hike and don't know where to put the trash from your lunch?

- You have a big project to do?

Signs of Success

Congratulations! You are practicing orderliness when you . . .

- Have a place to put each of your things

- Put them away in the same place whenever you are finished

- Have a plan before you start any job

- Solve problems step by step

- Create a harmonious space that makes your soul peaceful

- Appreciate the beauty and order of God's creation

Keep trying! You need more practice when you . . .

- Live with a mess

- Spend a lot of time looking for things

- Play it by ear—don't bother to plan

- Act confused or helpless when you have a problem

- Don't do anything to create beauty around you

- Disrespect Nature by littering or messing up

❧ *AFFIRMATION* ❧

I live this day with order, I do things step by step. I create beauty and harmony in my space and in my life.

❧ PATIENCE ❧

"O you who believe, seek courage in forti-
tude and prayer, for God is with those who
are patient and persevere."
—AL-QUR'AN 2:153

What Is Patience?

Patience is quiet hope and expectation based on trust that, in the end, everything will be all right. Patience means waiting. It is enduring a delay or troublesome situation without complaining.

It means having self-control because you can't control the way someone else is acting or when things don't go as you'd like. Patience is being calm and tolerant when difficult things happen.

Patience is persevering—sticking with something for as long as it takes to finish it. When you are patient, you know that things take time, just as a seed you plant will someday grow into a flower or a fruit-bearing tree. Patience is a commitment to the future. It is doing something now so that later something good will happen. It is also tolerating all of the things necessary to make it happen. Patience is seeing the end in the beginning—doing what you can and then calmly waiting, with trust that the results will come.

❧ ❧ ❧

Why Practice Patience?

Without patience people want everything now. They might plant a seed in the ground and want to eat the fruit right away. They have trouble doing things now which will have a result later, such as a project that takes a lot of work or going to school so that someday they can be a doctor or an artist or an engineer.

Without patience people can't stand to wait for anyone and fuss the whole time, which makes them and everyone else even more upset. When people are impatient, they act mad and irritable when things don't go their way or other people make mistakes.

When people practice patience, they do things now that will bear fruit in the future. They plant seeds so flowers, vegetables, and trees will grow. They study subjects that they will put to use ten years from now.

When people are patient, they don't whine, complain, or criticize. They forgive other people and themselves. They make the world a kind and gentle place, and other people feel safe around them.

How Do You Practice It?

You practice patience by accepting things you cannot control. Even if you feel impatient, you act calm and accepting while waiting for someone who is delayed. You have faith that things will turn out all right in the end. A sense of humor helps!

When you practice patience, you surrender to something that you have to endure, like an illness that will last a certain time, or a handicap you may always have, instead of fighting it and getting mad about it. You are gentle with others when they make mistakes, and you are gentle with yourself too.

Patience helps you to stick to something you are trying to do, even when it gets difficult or tiresome. You persevere until it is finished, even if there is no reward for all your work until the very end. You are willing to set goals for your future, knowing that it is really worth the effort.

Patience is having goals and picturing the end in the beginning. Trust in God can give you patience—a quiet hope that can get you through hard times.

What would patience look like if . . .

- Your mother is very late picking you up and you have been waiting a long time?

- You decide that you want to be a lawyer when you grow up?

- You want to grow some vegetables in your garden?

- You start to get annoyed when your sister forgets to put back something she borrowed from you?

- You wish you were taller?

- You have an illness which keeps you from playing your favorite sport?

Signs of Success

Congratulations! You are practicing patience when you . . .

- Calmly tolerate a delay or confusion

- Are willing to wait for things you want

- Set goals and stick with them until they are completed

- Do something now which will help you in the future

- Accept things you cannot control with humor and grace

- Are gentle with others when they make mistakes

- Rely on God to help you persevere

Keep trying! You need more practice when you . . .

- Think that everything you want should come right away

- Figure that if something takes time it is not worth it

- Get frustrated if things do not bear fruit right away

- Do only those things that have instant payoff

- Are irritable with others when they make a mistake or keep you waiting

- Don't trust God to help things turn out all right

❧ *AFFIRMATION* ❧

I am patient. I am gentle with others and myself when mistakes are made. I set goals and persevere until my goals are won. I trust God that all will be well.

❧ PEACEFULNESS ❦

"Blessed are the peacemakers: for they shall be called the children of God."
—MATTHEW 5:9

What Is Peacefulness?

Peacefulness is an inner sense of calm that can come in moments of silent gratitude or prayer. It is a way of becoming very quiet and looking at things so you can understand them. It is facing your fears and then letting them go. It is trusting that things will be all right.

Peacefulness is giving up the love of power for the power of love. It is practicing justice, which means to be fair to yourself and others. Peacefulness is a way of approaching conflict with others so no one is made wrong. Everyone wins because you work to find a peaceful solution. Peace comes when you give up violence, prejudice, and thinking of others as enemies.

Peacefulness comes from an awareness that all human beings are part of one human family. Peace in the world begins with peace in your heart and peace in your interactions with others.

Why Practice Peacefulness?

A peaceful heart is one which is free of trouble or worry. It allows you to trust. It is a quieting of your spirit, a willingness to enter your own inner stillness. Without peacefulness you feel that you have to control everyone and everything.

World peace is not only something that governments can create while all of us sit there waiting for them to do it. People make peace in their homes and schools and workplaces.

Peacefulness allows us to remain free of violence, free from prejudice, safe from injustice. When each of us is peaceful, all those who come in contact with us feel loved, respected, and treated fairly. Differences are seen as benefits rather than reasons to fight. The peace in our lives leads to peace in the world.

Without peacefulness we see differences as a threat to who and what we are. We judge others by what we have heard rather than by what we know, and look out for ourselves first even if others are hurt in the process. Without peace no one is safe. When there is violence, injustice, prejudice, or inequality, there is always fear and resentment. This can happen in a family or between nations. It leads to fights and wars. And no one ever really wins a war.

How Do You Practice It?

To be peaceful inside, become very still so that you can reflect, meditate, or pray. Give your worries to God and ask God to take care of them. When you do this every day, you become more and more peaceful.

To be a peacemaker, use peaceful language. Instead of saying, "I hate . . . ," calling people names, backbiting, or criticizing, use moderate language, even when you're angry. Talk about your anger: "It makes me angry when you come in my room without knocking." Speak softly and gently. Harm no one. Avoid hitting and other kinds of violence. Never, ever use weapons.

When you practice peacefulness, if you have a disagreement with someone, instead of attacking, making each other wrong, or using violent speech or actions, look for a peaceful solution. You can solve the problem so that both of you win. There are always lots of creative ways any problem can be solved. Violence never solves anything.

Look for the good in others. If something they do hurts or annoys you, forgive them right away. If they are violating your rights, stop them by reasonable, nonviolent means. Stand up for yourself and others. Appreciate differences instead of making them a cause for prejudice or fighting.

What would peacefulness look like if . . .

- Your brother bursts into your room and steps on a model or painting you just finished?

- There are children of another race and religion in your class and some of your classmates are making fun of them?

- You start to worry about a problem and find it is on your mind all the time?

- You decide to spend some time each day in contemplation or prayer?

- Some children start teasing you and asking you to fight?

Signs of Success

Congratulations! You are practicing peacefulness when you . . .

- Create inner peace, with a regular time to pray or meditate

- Give your worries to God and ask God's help in solving them

- Use peaceful language even when you are angry; speak softly and gently

- Avoid harming anyone

- When you disagree, find a peaceful solution

- Appreciate differences

- Give up the love of power for the power of love

Keep trying! You need more practice when you . . .

- Stay too busy to stop and pray

- Hit or speak harshly because you are angry

- Try to prove others wrong

- Get revenge if anyone hurts you, even accidentally

- Allow others to violate your rights

- Stick with your own group and avoid people who are different; have an us-against-them attitude

- Backbite or judge people by what you hear from others

❧ *AFFIRMATION* ☙

I use peaceful language and find peaceful solutions to any problem that arises. I find my inner peace and let it carry me gently through the day.

❧ PRAYERFULNESS ❧

"Call to me and I will answer you, and show you great and mighty things which you do not know." —JEREMIAH 33:3

What Is Prayerfulness?

Prayerfulness can be practiced in many ways. Prayer is talking with God. You can pray in silence or out loud. You can sing or dance in prayer. You can use any language. God always hears your thoughts and understands your heart.

Prayerfulness is living in a way which shows that you are in the presence of your Creator. It is doing simple things with an attitude of gratitude. It is knowing you are a unique creation of God, and are acting in ways which are worthy of that gift. Prayer is praising God, being thankful for things. Prayerfulness is quiet reflection. It is allowing the Great Spirit to speak to you. It is listening and receiving God's guidance.

You can turn to God in prayer at any time. You can share your hopes and problems, the things you feel ashamed of and the things you feel proud of. Prayerfulness is trusting God and turning things over to God. Prayerfulness is living your life with the awareness that it is a gift just to be alive.

Why Practice Prayerfulness?

People who rush around *doing* all the time without stopping to pray or reflect lose touch with their own spirits.

If we don't allow ourselves to feel the presence of God, we can get lonely even if we are in a crowd. Who else completely understands our worries, thoughts, hopes, and dreams?

We can pray any time, not just at special moments in a place of worship or when we see something beautiful in Nature.

Prayer makes things clear when we are confused, gives us hope when we are sad, gives us answers when we have a problem, and provides strength to face the challenges of life. With prayer we don't ever have to be alone.

How Do You Practice It?

You practice prayerfulness by becoming very still and turning to God. Let God know all that is in your heart, as if you were talking with your very best friend. Trust God's wisdom and don't expect that everything you ask will happen. Listen and notice what happens.

Without the listening part of prayer, it is like dialing someone's number on the telephone and then hanging up before they can answer you. Becoming very still and listening for an answer is a way to connect your spirit to the Great Spirit.

Prayer can be answered in many ways. A thought or idea may come to you while you are reflecting. You might have a dream that gives you an answer. You may be inspired by the actions or words of another person. You may start to see things differently. When you pray, be ready to receive an answer.

You can also pray by dedicating something you are doing to the Creator. It could be a simple chore, like making your bed, or doing some homework, or a special act of kindness to another person.

Prayerfulness is saying thank you to God and remembering to stay in God's presence. The feeling of love and connection does not have to stop when you finish praying. You can choose to stay with that feeling throughout the day.

What would prayerfulness look like if . . .

- You have a problem you don't want to talk to anyone about?

- You want to do something special for another person?

- You have been rushing around for days and realize you feel out of touch with God and yourself?

- You attend a service at your family's place of worship and wish you could keep that feeling?

- You are really happy about something that has happened?

Signs of Success

Congratulations! You are practicing prayerfulness when you . . .

- Take time every day to pray and reflect

- Talk to God as you would to a really good friend

- Share your innermost thoughts, hopes, and fears with God

- Ask God to provide you with what you need

- Trust, listen, and watch for God's answer

- Have an attitude of gratitude

- Dedicate some of your actions to God

Keep trying! You need more practice when you . . .

- Keep busy inside so you cannot talk or listen to God

- Pray only on special occasions

- Keep your thoughts, hopes, and fears to yourself

- Think God only helps others but not you

- Insist that God do what you think is best

- Let yourself feel helpless and alone

❊‖ *AFFIRMATION* ‖❊

Thank you, God, for the gift of prayer. Help me to live in Your presence. I will find Your answers in quiet moments. I dedicate my actions to You today.

❧ PURPOSEFULNESS ❧

"As long as the thoughts of an individual are scattered he will achieve no results, but if his thinking be concentrated on a single point wonderful will be the fruits thereof."
—SELECTED WRITINGS OF ABDU'L-BAHA

What Is Purposefulness?

Purposefulness is having a clear focus instead of being fuzzy or unsure what you're doing or why you're doing it. When you have a goal you are working toward, you are acting on purpose. To be purposeful means to concentrate on something. You concentrate your mind so that you can keep your goal before you. You concentrate your efforts so that something good will happen as a result. You are faithful to your purpose no matter what.

Some people just let things happen. A purposeful person *makes* things happen. With God's help, when you are purposeful, you can achieve just about anything.

❧ ❧ ❧

Why Practice Purposefulness?

Unless you are purposeful, you will become confused. You will lose track of what you are doing, let yourself get distracted, and your efforts will be lost. Without a sense of purpose you wouldn't know the reasons why you are doing something, and when the going gets tough you would just give up.

Without a clear purpose you would probably become scattered. Without concentrated efforts nothing gets accomplished. You would do a little of this and a little of that, never really finishing anything. You would be surrounded by all kinds of unfinished projects with none of them really complete. All your time and effort would be wasted.

When you choose to be purposeful, you can accomplish great things. You have a vision or goal for what you want to do. Act in a concentrated and focused way, and you will see the results of your efforts. You will always be motivated because you know why you are doing something. You will stick to your purpose no matter what happens.

How Do You Practice It?

Being purposeful begins with a vision of what you want to do. You are purposeful when you decide to do something that matters to you or someone important to you. It could be God.

Before you start something, ask yourself, "What do I really want to accomplish?" This is your vision and your goal. Then ask yourself, "What makes this so important to me?" The answer to this is your purpose. Now you are ready to act.

As you act, keep asking yourself, "Is what I am doing going to help me accomplish my purpose?" If the answer is yes, then concentrate really hard on doing it. If the answer is no, then change what you are doing to fit your purpose.

If something comes along to distract you, try hard to resist it. Get back to your purpose as soon as you can.

Do things one at a time, with as much care and concentration as you can. Don't let yourself get scattered in many directions, trying to do everything at once.

What would purposefulness look like if . . .

- You decide to build or create something that is difficult?

- You are trying to finish your homework and keep getting distracted by daydreaming?

- A friend comes over while you are doing your chores?

- You start to feel scattered doing too many things at once?

- You want to learn to play an instrument?

- You find it is really hard to practice a virtue?

Signs of Success

Congratulations! You are practicing purposefulness when you . . .

- Have a clear vision of what you want to accomplish

- Think about why you want to accomplish it

- Concentrate your efforts on your goals

- Keep from getting scattered or distracted

- Do things one at a time and finish what you start

- Get back to your purpose if you do get distracted

- Persevere until you get results

Keep trying! You need more practice when you . . .

- Decide that nothing matters

- Get so excited that you start off in many directions at once

- Forget what you are doing

- Forget your reasons for doing it

- Change your goals to make things easier for yourself

- Quit before you have accomplished what you set out to do

❧ *AFFIRMATION* ❧

I am purposeful. I am clear about what I am doing and why. I concentrate on what is most important. With God's help I can accomplish great things.

❧ RELIABILITY ☙

*"**L**ike a beautiful flower, full of color but without scent, are the fair but fruitless words of one who does not act accordingly.*

"Like a beautiful flower, full of color and full of scent, are the pure and fruitful words of one who acts accordingly."
—DHAMMAPADA 51–52

What Is Reliability?

Reliability means that others can depend on you. It is doing something that you have agreed to do in a predictable way, without forgetting or having to be reminded. People don't have to wonder if it will get done.

When you are practicing reliability, others can count on you to do your best to keep your commitments. If there is any way at all to keep a promise you have made, you will do it, even if it is difficult and your perseverance is tested. You really care about doing what you said you would. Other people can relax, knowing it is in your reliable hands.

❧ ❧ ❧

Why Practice Reliability?

When people are unreliable, others can't trust them. If people do what they are supposed to do sometimes and other times not, we can never know for sure if they will do what they promise, even if it is something really important. This creates anxiety and distrust. If someone forgets to pick up the food for dinner, everyone goes hungry.

If airplanes, trains, or buses are late, passengers miss important appointments. If people who build houses or bridges or toys can't be relied on to build them properly, others suffer when they fall apart.

When you practice reliability, you treat any job as a sacred trust. Others can count on you to do your job in a dependable way. It makes a big difference in the safety and sense of peacefulness in other people's lives. When you are reliable, people can trust you to do your part.

How Do You Practice It?

You practice reliability by making agreements you can keep. You agree to do things that others count on. Then you do everything in your power to see that the agreement is kept. You make sure that what you have promised gets done—unless it was impossible because of things beyond your control.

When you are older and have responsibilities such as raising a child or painting a house or practicing medicine or putting out fires, if you are practicing reliability, you will give your best effort to your job. You can begin practicing reliability now by taking your responsibilities seriously—like a sacred trust, an important commitment.

You practice reliability by planning ahead. You know what you are to do and how to do it. You leave enough time to do it. Be sure that you start in plenty of time. Do your best. Then finish on time. If something interferes and your original idea for how to do it is interrupted, try to think of another way to get it done. Being reliable is one of the best ways to be of service.

What would reliability look like if . . .

- You agreed to come home by a certain time and a friend invites you to do something fun?

- It is your turn to do the dishes and you're not in the mood?

- You promised your mom you would brush your teeth after breakfast and you're worried about missing the bus?

- Some friends are building a clubhouse and you agreed to bring the nails, but you discover your parents don't have any?

- Your part of a team report is due tomorrow and you feel too sleepy to finish it?

Signs of Success

Congratulations! You are practicing reliability when you . . .

- Agree to do things that help others

- Make promises you can keep

- Treat your agreements seriously

- Plan ahead

- Do your best

- Finish on time

- If obstacles occur, find another way to keep your promise

Keep trying! You need more practice when you . . .

- Avoid taking responsibility

- Forget what you were supposed to do

- Are usually late

- Don't plan ahead—scramble to do things at the last minute

- Have to be reminded

- Give up easily if you meet an obstacle

- Make excuses when you fail

❧ *AFFIRMATION* ☙

I am reliable. I keep my promises. Others can count on me. Nothing can stop me from giving my best.

⇢ RESPECT ⇠

> "*A man is not an elder because his head is gray . . . he in whom truth, virtue, gentleness, self-control, moderation, he who is steadfast and free from impurity, is rightly called an elder . . . is called respectable.*"
> —DHAMMAPADA 260–263

What Is Respect?

Respect is an attitude of honoring people and caring about their rights. Being respectful is reflected in the courtesy with which we treat one another, the way we speak, and the way we treat other people's belongings. Speaking and acting respectfully gives people the dignity they deserve.

It is particularly important to be respectful of elders, like your parents, grandparents, and teachers. Because they have lived longer, they have wisdom and can teach you many things. While everyone deserves respect, elders deserve a special measure of courtesy and respect.

Respect includes honoring the rules of your family and your school, behaving in a way which makes life more peaceful and orderly.

Being respectful includes self-respect. This means that you protect your rights, such as privacy and modesty. If anyone violates your rights, even if it is an elder, this must be stopped. Every woman, man, and child was created by God, and we all deserve respect.

Why Practice Respect?

Without respectfulness people's privacy would be violated. Anyone who felt like it would read a private letter or diary, or walk into the washroom or bedroom when you want to be alone. Without respect people speak rudely to each other and treat others as if they don't matter. Without self-respect you would let others use you or hurt you.

Being respectful helps people feel valued. Elders deserve special respect because they have lived longer and learned many of life's lessons.

Without respect for elders, children would do exactly as they please. Without respect for laws or rules, we would just have chaos. Think of what it would be like to ride in a car if none of the other drivers respected the rules of the road.

When you respect other people's property, they are more likely to respect yours. When you treat yourself with respect, others respect you too.

How Do You Practice It?

A good way to practice respect is to think about how you would like to be treated and then treat others that way. How would you like others to treat your belongings, your right to privacy, your need for dignity? If you feel like using someone else's things, you ask rather than just taking. You don't run around inside someone's home when there are breakables there. You treat their space and their belongings with respect.

Being respectful is expressing even your strongest feelings in a peaceful way. Respect is speaking quietly and courteously, especially to elders. It is not interrupting but saying, "Excuse me," and then waiting for someone to give you his attention. It is expressing your opinion as an opinion, respectful of the fact that there is more than one way of seeing things.

Practicing self-respect is treating yourself as you feel others deserve to be treated. You deserve it too!

What would respect look like if . . .

- You want to use your friend's bike but she is not around to ask?

- Your grandparents come over and start giving you some advice?

- You find yourself talking back to your mother?

- Your brother is in the washroom and you need to ask him a question?

- There is a rule at school you don't agree with?

- An older person starts touching you inappropriately?

Signs of Success

Congratulations! You are practicing respect when you . . .

- Treat everyone the way you would like to be treated

- Treat the property of others with special care

- Honor other people's need for time and space to themselves

- Speak courteously to everyone

- Are receptive to the wisdom of elders

- Honor the rules of your family and nation

- Expect respect for your body and your rights

Keep trying! You need more practice when you . . .

- Treat others like they don't matter

- Ignore the wisdom of elders

- Use anything you want without the owner's permission

- Interrupt or barge in on anyone

- Make fun or talk back to elders

- Disobey the rules of your family or school

- Allow others to treat you disrespectfully

❧ *AFFIRMATION* ☙

I am respectful. I treat others and myself as we deserve to be treated. I show courtesy to everyone. I learn from the wisdom of my elders.

❧ RESPONSIBILITY ❧

> "*He who finds the right path does so for himself; and he who goes astray does so to his own loss; and no one who carries a burden bears another's load.*"
>
> —AL-QUR'AN 17:15

What Is Responsibility?

Being responsible means that others can depend on you. Being responsible means to do something well and to the best of your ability. Being responsible is being willing to be accountable for what you do or not do. You accept credit when you do things right (humbly, of course!), and you accept correction when things go wrong.

When you are responsible, you keep your agreements. If you agree to do something for your family or for a friend, you don't put it off or forget about it. You make sure it gets done. Being responsible is the ability to respond ably.

When you make a mistake, you take responsibility for it. You don't blame the weather, someone else, or your memory ("I forgot!"). If something goes wrong, you may give an explanation for why things happened the way they did, but you make no excuses. When you take responsibility, you are telling others that they can count on you. Being responsible is a sign of growing up.

Why Practice Responsibility?

When you take responsibility for your own actions, others can count on you. When you are willing to be accountable, you get a lot of things done, and people feel they can trust you. When something goes right or wrong, people like to know who to thank or who to go to in order to make things right. When you act responsibly, people know they can do this with you.

When people are not willing to be responsible, things they have agreed to do may never get done. Homework is forgotten, promises are not kept, jobs are left undone, and others become disappointed.

People who makes excuses instead of taking responsibility keep making the same mistakes. Others begin to wonder if they are trustworthy.

Others would like to depend on us. If we are responsible, then they can.

How Do You Practice It?

When you agree to do something, whether it is homework, a job, or watching your little brother, you take it seriously, like a sacred trust. You take responsibility for things you can do. You don't agree to do things which are too hard or that you don't really have time for. Taking on too much responsibility and then not doing it is irresponsible.

When you act responsibly, you do things as well as you possibly can. If it isn't just right, and a mistake is made, you don't act defensive. You are ready and willing to clear up misunderstandings.

You accept credit for doing things well and correction when things go wrong. You listen carefully, accept responsibility, and do what you can to make it right.

What would responsibility look like if . . .

- You are given a job to do at home and you'd rather read or watch TV?

- You are given a lot of homework at school?

- You just broke something in your home?

- You promised your friend you'd meet her right after school, but then remember you have to get to a music lesson?

- You are watching your little brother in a store while your mother finishes shopping?

Signs of Success

Congratulations! You are practicing responsibility when you . . .

- Respond ably by doing things to the best of your ability

- Focus on your own part, not someone else's

- Are willing to accept credit or correction

- Are ready and willing to clear up misunderstanding

- Admit mistakes without making excuses

- Take on new responsibilities when you are ready

Keep trying! You need more practice when you . . .

- Don't keep your agreements

- Agree to do things that are beyond your ability

- Don't listen to what people tell you about what you have done unless it's good

- Focus on what others are supposed to be doing

- Make excuses for your mistakes

- Do things just so-so

- Take on nothing unless you are forced to

❧ *AFFIRMATION* ❧

I am responsible. I give my best to all that I do and keep my agreements. I welcome both praise and correction for my actions.

❧ REVERENCE ❧

"May Obedience conquer disobedience within this house, and may peace triumph over discord here, and generous giving over avarice, reverence over contempt, speech with truthful words over lying utterance."
—YASNA 60:5

What Is Reverence?

Reverence is behaving with an awareness that you are always in the presence of the Creator and that all life is precious. Reverence can be experienced in moments of prayer or reflection. It is treating holy books and other sacred things as very special.

Reverence is showing respect. It is being careful to honor the gifts of life, including other people.

Whether you are in a place of worship or spending time in a place of beauty, reverence is being still and allowing the wonder you feel to shine through.

🌱 🌱 🌱

Why Practice Reverence?

Reverence is a quality of the spirit. It allows you to feel the presence of the Creator. If you don't treat things which are sacred to you as they deserve, then the most important things become the same as the most ordinary things.

If you had no reverence for living things, you would treat them carelessly instead of revering them as part of God's creation. If you are too rushed or impatient, unable to become still and listen to your heart, you miss one of the most special parts of life.

God's love is like rain. It falls everywhere. But it can only be received if you hold out your hands and create a space to receive it. Reverence allows you to feel God's love.

How Do You Practice It?

Reverence can be experienced in times of prayer, meditation, or communion. Everyone needs regular time for reflection. It is the best way for each of us to hear the wisdom which comes from deep inside. Reverence is choosing not to think of anything else. You concentrate your whole being on the sacredness of that moment. Reverence allows you to listen to your heart.

Reverence means entering a time of worship in a quiet, respectful way. Reverence can be expressed in daily acts of kindness for others, especially the people you are closest to. Even a simple act can be sacred if you do it with reverence.

Reverence is an attitude of deep respect for living things. It is taking responsibility by caring for the earth and all the gifts you receive from it, doing your part to keep it clean and healthy. Reverence comes when you allow yourself to experience beauty. Giving yourself time to enjoy the wonder of nature is one of the best ways to feel your own reverence.

What would reverence look like if . . .

- You walk into a room and notice someone is praying?

- You enter a place of worship?

- You are hiking in a place of natural beauty?

- You realize you haven't stopped to reflect for a long time?

- You find out that the water near your home is getting polluted?

- You find yourself treating your mother disrespectfully?

Signs of Success

Congratulations! You are practicing reverence when you . . .

- Have an attitude of deep respect toward all living things

- Have a regular practice of reflection or prayer

- Treat sacred things with special care

- Act as if you are in the presence of the Creator

- Do your part to care for the earth

- Spend time in the beauty of nature

Keep trying! You need more practice when you . . .

- Act as if nothing is special or sacred

- Avoid reflection. Stay too busy to practice inner stillness.

- Treat everything the same and nothing with respect

- Act as if people don't really matter to you

- Forget to care responsibly for the earth and its gifts

❧ AFFIRMATION ☙

I am practicing reverence. I take time today to be still, to reflect, and to listen to my heart. I act with respect toward all beings.

❧ SELF-DISCIPLINE ❧

> "*Discipline, to be sure, is never pleasant; at times it seems painful, but afterward those who have been trained by it reap the harvest of a peaceful and upright life.*"
> —HEBREWS 12:11

What Is Self-discipline?

Discipline means control. Self-discipline is self-control. It means getting yourself to do what you really want to do rather than being a leaf in the wind of your thoughts or feelings. Self-discipline means choosing to do what you feel is right. It is bringing order and efficiency into your life.

With self-discipline you can be moderate. You don't overdo things or let yourself become too lazy. You get things done. Feelings and thoughts come and go. You may not be able to control your thoughts and feelings, but you can control what you do with them. You don't lose control of yourself when you are hurt or angry but decide how you are going to talk and what you are going to do.

When you are self-disciplined, you create structure in your life, like practicing the trumpet or brushing your teeth every single night. You don't procrastinate. With self-discipline you take charge of yourself.

Why Practice Self-discipline?

When you have self-discipline, you are controlling your own behavior so others don't have to. Self-discipline brings you freedom. You get things done efficiently, so you don't have to scramble at the last minute or feel burdened by all the tasks that are waiting. Procrastination (putting things off until the last minute) is a very heavy burden.

When people lack self-discipline, they lose control of their emotions. Other people get hurt or upset, and the undisciplined person gets into trouble. Without self-discipline life is helter-skelter. You never know what you will do next.

When you practice self-discipline, no one has to watch you or control you, because you are watching yourself and exercising self-control. You get to decide what you will do rather than waiting for people to make you do it.

How Do You Practice It?

Detachment is a big help when you want to practice self-discipline. You watch yourself, think about things and choose how you are going to behave. For example, if you get angry, you always have a choice. You can yell, hit someone, or do something else which will hurt others and yourself. Or you can choose to feel your anger, then use your quiet voice to tell someone you are angry and why. They are much more likely to want to make things better than if you lost your temper.

You practice self-discipline by creating routines for yourself. You may want to have a prayer and reflection time each day, take a bath at a certain time, have a certain time to play, do your homework or your chores. You put limits on yourself such as the amount of television you watch or the cookies you eat, so you have enough but not too much.

When you have self-discipline, you choose to follow the rules of your family and school and can actually enjoy it.

With self-discipline you are free of procrastination and greed. You use your head to help you deal with your emotions. Your life is more peaceful.

What would self-discipline look like if . . .

- You have put off doing a big job for some time?

- You are really angry when your brother starts wrestling with you?

- Your family has a rule of only three cookies after school, but no one is watching?

- You notice you are watching too much TV and feeling lazy?

- You decide you need a new daily routine?

- You keep getting punished for breaking a rule?

Signs of Success

Congratulations! You are practicing self-discipline when you . . .

- Use detachment so your emotions won't control you

- Speak and act calmly when you are hurt or angry

- Get things done in an orderly and efficient way

- Create structure in your life

- Do what is expected without people having to watch you

- Do things on time

Keep trying! You need more practice when you . . .

- Lose your temper or get carried away by your emotions

- Have no plan for how to do things

- Do whatever you feel like doing

- Behave well only when you are being watched

- Disregard the rules

- Usually procrastinate

✢ *AFFIRMATION* ✢

I have self-discipline. I use my time well and get things done. I choose my actions with detachment.

❧ SERVICE ❧

"Devote thyself to My service, do all thine acts for My sake, and thou shalt attain the goal." —BHAGAVAD-GITA 12:10

What Is Service?

Service is giving to others and wanting to make a difference in the lives of others. Helping other people is one of the best ways to serve God.

Having an attitude of service means looking for ways to be of help rather than waiting to be asked. The needs of others are as important to you as your own. When you are service-oriented, you anticipate people's needs and then think of ways to help them.

You do things for other people just to be helpful, not because you hope they will pay you or reward you. You do things just because you care.

When you work with a spirit of service, you give a job your best effort. You don't just do the least amount possible. You make a real contribution.

❧ ❧ ❧

Why Practice Service?

If people didn't care about serving one another, everyone would be on his own. If someone was in trouble or needed help, no one would be there to help unless she was going to be paid or had some selfish motive.

Without a desire to be of service, people have to be pushed or nagged to do their part.

With an attitude of service, we create love and happiness around us. Others feel cared for. They can depend on us to be responsive when something needs to be taken care of.

We do our work with heart. We give it our best. When people are service-oriented, they accomplish everything that needs to be done without anyone having to ask. People who want to be of service can change the world.

How Do You Practice It?

When you want to be service-oriented, watch other people to see what help they might need. Then do something to help. Look for little ways to make life easier or happier for others. If someone looks lost or lonely, go up and ask if you can help. Think of little ways to serve your family by doing extra chores or just doing thoughtful little things.

You can do things to serve the earth by remembering to recycle, reduce the things you use, and reuse old things—instead of always buying new ones. You could make a compost pile in your backyard or plant a tree where one has been cut down. When you focus on service, there are always lots of wonderful things you can do—things which will make a difference in the world.

When you work, do it with a spirit of service. Give it the best you can. Do it for the sake of God. Remember that God placed us here to take care of one another and the earth.

What would an attitude of service look like if . . .

- It is raining outside and your mother is coming up the road with no umbrella?

- You have a job to do for your family?

- You wonder how you can serve the world when you grow up?

- You notice your family throws away a lot of garbage?

- A new student in your school looks a little lost?

- Your teacher is struggling to carry a lot of materials?

Signs of Success

Congratulations! You are being of service when you . . .

- Want to make a difference in the world

- Look for opportunities to be of service

- Think of thoughtful things to do to help your family and friends

- Work with enthusiasm

- Don't wait to be asked when something needs doing

- Do your part to recycle, reduce, or reuse

Keep trying! You need more practice when you . . .

- Ignore people who need help

- See something that needs doing and hope someone else does it

- See someone who is lost and ignore them

- Expect others to always serve you

- Do a job only for the hope of reward

- Don't think your efforts can make any difference

⇥ AFFIRMATION ⇤

I look for opportunities to be of service. I do not wait to be asked. I am thoughtful of others. I make a difference in the world.

❦ STEADFASTNESS ❧

"My heart is steadfast, O God, my heart is steadfast."
—PSALMS 57:8

What Is Steadfastness?

Steadfastness is being steady and dependable, sticking with something no matter what. Do you know the story about the tortoise and the hare? Even though the tortoise was very slow compared to the rabbit, he won the race by being steadfast. He kept on going.

Steadfastness is being faithful and purposeful. Steadfastness is remaining true to someone or something in spite of any tests or obstacles that appear to stop you. When you are steadfast, you commit yourself to something for however long it may take.

🌱 🌱 🌱

Why Practice Steadfastness?

Without steadfastness people waver. They can be enthusiastic one minute and doubtful the next. They may finish something they agreed to do or they may forget about it. It depends how many doubts they have or how hard it becomes to keep their commitments. You never know what you can count on with someone who is not practicing steadfastness.

When we are steadfast, even when we have doubts, in our hearts we remain committed. When we are steadfast we can shrug off the doubts because down deep we know where we stand and are committed for the long run. Others are reassured by the strength and dependability of our commitment. With steadfastness we keep moving forward.

How Do You Practice It?

You practice steadfastness by being committed. You need to decide if something is worthy of your commitment. Think about it and then decide. You need to know before you start that you are in this until it is finished.

Then pace yourself. When you practice steadfastness, you keep a steady pace, and remain constant no matter what. If you are doing a job, keep at it without going too fast to tire yourself out or too slow to get it done on time. Just put one foot in front of the other and keep on going. If you are steadfast in learning something new, you stick with it even when you wonder if you will ever understand. Get whatever help you need to keep going.

If you are a steadfast friend, you stick by your friends even when they aren't much fun, they need a lot of attention, or they are going through a hard time.

When you find yourself wondering, "Can I really do this?" or "Is it really worth all this effort?" steadfastness helps you to accept your doubts and do it anyway.

You are like a strong ship in a storm. You don't let yourself become battered or blown off course. You just ride the waves.

What would steadfastness look like if . . .

- You have been friends with someone for a long time and you begin to feel bored?

- You are in the middle of a hard job and start feeling tired?

- You have spent a lot of time practicing a sport, dance, or art and begin to wonder if you can really succeed?

- Your family is hiking to the top of a mountain and you don't think you can make it?

- You have a new chore and are afraid you will forget to do it?

- Your best friend moves away and you don't want to forget her?

Signs of Success

Congratulations! You are practicing steadfastness when you . . .

- Think about whether you really want to commit to something or someone

- Pace yourself. Go at a rate you can maintain.

- Take it one step at a time, remaining steady

- Don't let doubts or tests blow you off course

- Stand by your friends and loved ones

- Ask God to help keep you steadfast

Keep trying! You need more practice when you . . . .

- Don't make commitments

- Just do what is easiest at the moment

- Do things just until they become difficult

- Give in to your doubts

- Don't finish things that are difficult

- Speed up or slow down too much

❧ AFFIRMATION ❧

I am steadfast. I keep a steady pace in what I choose to do. I keep on keeping on. I am a loyal and committed friend.

⊰❈ TACT ❈⊱

"A soft answer turns away wrath, but a grievous word stirs up anger."
—PROVERBS 15:1

What Is Tact?

Tact is telling the truth in a way that does not disturb or offend people. It is knowing what to say and what is better left unsaid. Being tactful is sharing your news with others in a way that makes it easier for them to accept it.

Tact is thinking before you speak. Being tactful means knowing when to stay silent.

Often you know things that you could say, but saying them may hurt someone. Rather than tell a lie, being tactful means that you look for a way to share the truth so that it helps rather than hurts the other person. This is especially important when you feel angry or upset.

When you are tactful, you don't point out people's differences to embarrass them. You are as careful about others' feelings as you would like them to be of yours.

🌱 🌱 🌱

Why Practice Tact?

When people do not practice tact, they are rude and blunt. They go around saying whatever pops into their heads. Other people's feelings are hurt.

Without tact people are insensitive to others. They don't wait to be asked a question. They may tell the truth, but they do it in a way which is too painful for others to hear. Other people get their guard up, and nothing much comes out of the conversation except hurt.

Without tact, when people are angry, they say things which can damage a relationship.

When people are being tactful, the truth is always told with gentleness and kindness. People wait to be asked before sharing anything that may be hurtful. Even if they are angry, tactful people avoid saying mean things. Other people can listen more easily, and so problems can be worked out.

We all grow and learn when the truth is presented to us with tact.

How Do You Practice It?

You practice tact by being kind when you tell the truth. Stop and think before you speak, asking yourself if this is something better left unsaid. Decide whether to keep quiet or speak up. Sometimes being tactful is keeping things to yourself when telling others might hurt them. If you do speak up, do it in a way which is sensitive to another's feelings. Don't do it in front of other people or in a way that will embarrass them.

If someone asks you a direct question and you think the answer might hurt him, to think of a tactful answer say "Let me think" and then take your time. This is also important when you feel angry. Rather than just attacking someone with your words, wait until you can calmly tell them what is bothering you in an objective way.

When you practice tactfulness, you don't draw attention to someone who looks different. You don't point and laugh, and you don't look away as if he is ugly. You just smile and say hello the way you would with anyone.

When you are really good at practicing tact, you can tell someone almost anything and he will feel good about having heard it.

What would tact look like if . . .

- You meet someone who has a handicap?

- You feel really mad at your brother about something?

- You get upset in school when your teacher does something you think is unfair?

- Your friend asks you if you like her strange haircut?

- While you are with a group of friends, you notice that someone's pants are unzipped?

- You are hugging your father and notice he has bad breath?

Signs of Success

Congratulations! You are practicing tact when you . . .

- Think before you speak

- Decide if it is better to tell the truth or keep silent

- Often keep an unpleasant or critical thought to yourself

- Become sensitive to other people's feelings

- Tell the truth kindly and gently

- Treat people who look different as you would treat anyone

Keep trying! You need more practice when you . . .

- Say whatever pops into your mind

- Embarrass people in front of others

- Tell people everything you think whether you are asked or not

- Do not think about the feelings of others

- Speak without caring that your words may hurt

- Say hurtful things when you are angry

❧ *AFFIRMATION* ❦

I act with tact. I think before I speak. I am considerate of other people's feelings. I tell the truth kindly and gently.

❧⊱ THANKFULNESS ⊰❧

"What is to come is better for you than what has gone before: For your Lord will certainly give you, and you will be content. . . . Keep recounting the favors of your Lord."
—AL-QUR'AN 93

What Is Thankfulness?

Thankfulness is being grateful for what you have. It is an attitude of gratitude for learning, loving, and being. Thankfulness is being glad for the special things which come along. It is also being grateful for the little things which happen around you and within you every day. It is an openness and willingness to receive each of God's bounties.

To be thankful is to have a sense of wonder about the beauty of this world and to welcome all of life as a gift. Thankfulness is a path to contentment.

Thankfulness is a way to get perspective when things don't look good and you start to lose hope. It is a way to grow when painful things happen, by looking at the gifts which are always there, even when they seem hidden.

❧ ❧ ❧

Why Practice Thankfulness?

Without thankfulness people would stay focused on negativity. They would do nothing but whine and complain. They would miss the beauty of life and the power of learning, especially during difficult times.

No matter how difficult or dark things become, there is always light. There is something to learn in every painful situation. In fact, sometimes when you look back at a really hard test in your life and realize what you learned, that is when you feel the most grateful of all.

Thanksgiving is conducive to bounty. When you open your heart by giving thanks to the Creator, you create more room for the flow of good things to come. Thankfulness leads to optimism. And when you expect the best, you often find it.

How Do You Practice It?

You practice thankfulness by noticing the beauty around you and within you. Then let yourself feel the gratitude in your heart.

Count your blessings often, especially when you are having a hard time. Find the lessons in all things, for they are the true gifts of this life. Avoid envy because it can destroy your trust. The moment you envy someone else, you are rejecting the gifts that are yours.

If you want to practice thankfulness, learn to receive. It is blessed to give, and it is blessed to receive. Everyone needs to have the opportunity to give, including the people who care for you. Be optimistic by being receptive to life rather than allowing fear or worry to control you.

To practice thankfulness, appreciate little things—a flower by the road, the stars at night, a challenge met, a laugh with a friend, a sorrow shared. To be truly thankful, don't wait for a dream to be fulfilled. Celebrate the moment.

What would thankfulness look like if . . .

- You feel sad and defeated because of many problems?

- You wish you were more like the most popular person you know?

- You go for a walk in a place of beauty?

- You have a painful experience and wonder why God allowed it to happen?

- Someone gives you a gift?

Signs of Success

Congratulations! You are practicing thankfulness when you . . .

- Have an attitude of gratitude

- Are receptive to gifts

- Appreciate your own abilities instead of envying others

- See the difficulties of your life as opportunities to learn

- Expect the best

- Appreciate the beauty of this earth

- Count your blessings every day

- Offer thanks to the Creator

Keep trying! You need more practice when you . . .

- Expect the worst

- Often feel like a victim

- Envy the gifts of others and feel less than they

- Fail to notice beauty

- Forget to learn the lessons in every situation

- Take your life for granted

- Don't thank God for the gifts in your life

❧ AFFIRMATION ❧

I am thankful for the many gifts within me and around me today. I celebrate each moment by opening myself to beauty and to learning. I expect the best.

❧ TOLERANCE ❧

> *"Be tolerant with one another and forgiving, if any of you has cause for complaint: you must forgive as the Lord forgave you."*
> —COLOSSIANS 3:13

What Is Tolerance?

Tolerance is being able to accept things that you wish were different. If you are practicing tolerance and someone annoys you, you just go on and don't pay too much attention.

When you practice tolerance, you can be flexible. Some people find it difficult to tolerate any change in the way they want things to be. They fuss and fume if it is too hot or cold, too noisy or too quiet, or something is taking too long.

When you practice tolerance, you don't expect others to think, look, or act just like you. You accept differences. You overlook the faults of others, especially of people in your own family.

When you are practicing tolerance, you are able to sort out what is important from what is not. You show patience and forgiveness when people make mistakes. You accept what you cannot change with good grace.

Why Practice Tolerance?

People who don't practice tolerance cannot stand to have anything differ from what they want or expect. They criticize, complain, and condemn people for doing things they don't like or even for being different. They try to change other people rather than overlooking their faults. They have difficulty forgiving. Without tolerance people are unhappy most of the time, and people around them become unhappy too.

Tolerance gives us the power to stick with a situation even when it gets uncomfortable. It gives us flexibility.

When people are practicing tolerance, there is space to be and space to grow. If there is something we don't like about each other, we overlook it out of love or friendship. This gives us all an opportunity to work on ourselves because we want to and not because we have to. When we are tolerant, we don't allow differences to drive us apart.

How Do You Practice It?

When you practice tolerance, you have the patience and flexibility to live with things you don't like. You don't expect others to be just like you. You accept differences. You don't judge others because they look different from you.

When things are uncomfortable and cannot be changed, you accept them with good grace instead of complaining.

You forgive others instead of holding a grudge or wishing and wishing they would change. If you don't like something about a relationship, instead of trying to change the other person, you focus on changing yourself. When you are tolerant, you can agree to disagree with someone. You don't insist on her seeing it your way. Tolerance does not mean being passive when someone is unjust or abusive.

Practicing tolerance is asking God to help you accept the things you cannot change.

What would tolerance look like if . . .

- Your sister has a really annoying habit she can't seem to change?

- You're on a long trip with your parents and it is very hot and uncomfortable?

- Your friend and you disagree about whose dog is the smartest?

- Your mother picks you up late for the third time this week?

- A child in your class keeps stealing your pencils?

- You meet someone with a strange accent?

Signs of Success

Congratulations! You are practicing tolerance when you . . .

- Are open to differences

- Are free of prejudice

- Don't complain when uncomfortable conditions can't be helped

- Forgive others instead of holding a grudge

- Focus on changing yourself when a relationship isn't right

- Overlook people's faults

- Ask God to help you accept the things you cannot change

Keep trying! You need more practice when you . . .

- Believe that all differences cause trouble

- Try to get everyone to think and act like you

- Try to change other people

- Can't take discomfort without complaining

- Accept injustice or abuse

- Keep trying to change things which will never change

❧ *AFFIRMATION* ❧

I am tolerant. I overlook people's faults. I am open to differences. God help me to accept the things I cannot change.

⊱ ❀ TRUST ❀ ⊰

"Trust in the Lord and he will guide you aright. One who has this trust need fear nothing. He can be at perfect peace and happiness, for he will be guided aright."
—MAHAVAGGA 8.15.13

What Is Trust?

Trust is having faith. It is relying and believing in someone or something. It is having confidence that the right thing will come about without trying to control it or make it happen, just as you trust the sun to rise in the morning without having to do a single thing.

Trusting others is believing that people will do what they say without having to get them to do it. Trusting yourself is having faith in your own capacity to learn and grow.

Sometimes it is hard to trust when life brings painful experiences. Trust doesn't mean to expect life to be easy all the time.

Trust is being sure, deep down, that there is some gift or learning in everything life brings, and that God's love is always with you. When you have trust, you know that you are never alone.

Why Practice Trust?

Without trust you always feel like you have to control things to make them turn out right. Even things that you cannot control start to worry you. Can you imagine having a good night's sleep if you were worrying that if you didn't do something about it, the sun would not rise in the morning?

Trusting others leaves you free to concentrate on those things that *you* need to do. You do not waste energy worrying about the things that other people are doing.

Trusting yourself is an important part of growing. If you didn't trust yourself, you would worry over every mistake instead of just doing your best and trusting it to be enough.

Trusting God allows you to receive and follow the guidance to do what is right for you.

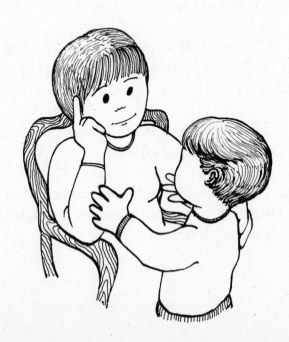

How Do You Practice It?

Trust comes when you are willing to rely on God, yourself, and others. By having basic confidence that things will go right, you help things to work out right.

When you trust, fear goes away. Even when difficult or sad things happen, trusting God means you believe there is a good reason for what is happening, that it can help you grow stronger or learn something new. When you are practicing trust, you relax about things turning out all right. Instead of worrying, you let your fears come and then you let them go, like leaves passing in a stream.

When someone makes a promise, trusting him means that you go ahead and make plans based on his promise, without reminding, nagging, or trying to control him.

People who keep breaking promises and agreements are not worthy of trust. It is foolish to keep trusting them, and it doesn't serve them well. Start trusting them only when they choose to be trustworthy.

What would trust look like if . . .

- You're having trouble in a relationship?

- A friend makes a promise to you?

- You start to worry that it's going to rain on your picnic?

- A person who has lost your things in the past wants to borrow your favorite music tape?

- You start to feel really scared about something bad happening?

- You make a mistake?

Signs of Success

Congratulations! You are practicing trust when you . . .

- Believe there is some good in everything that happens

- Look for the gift or lesson in painful experiences

- Let trust chase away your fears

- Know that your best is good enough

- Trust others unless you have good reasons not to

- Don't nag, worry, or try to take control

Keep trying! You need more practice when you . . .

- Let fear control your life

- Worry about things before they happen

- Don't trust yourself because you make mistakes

- Nag or try to control others on whom you are relying

- Keep trusting someone who has shown they are unworthy of trust

- Fail to forgive someone who is ready to be trustworthy

⊰ *AFFIRMATION* ⊱

I trust God that there is some good in everything that happens. I have no need to control others. All fear and worry are released. I feel at peace, and know I am not alone.

TRUSTWORTHINESS

"When you make a vow to God, do not delay to fulfill it. For he has no pleasure in fools; what you vow, fulfill. It is better not to vow at all than to vow and not fulfill."
—ECCLESIASTES 5:34

What Is Trustworthiness?

Trustworthiness means you can be counted on. When you are trustworthy, if you make a promise or a vow, you keep your word no matter how hard it becomes.

When you are practicing trustworthiness, others can rely on you. They can trust that if it is at all possible, you will do what you said you would.

Being trustworthy means that if someone asks you to do something, and you start out to do it, you will finish it (and do your best) even if it becomes really hard.

People who practice trustworthiness are known for their determination, their reliability, and their truthfulness. They keep their word. Others know they can be trusted.

Why Practice Trustworthiness?

Without trustworthiness, agreements and promises don't mean anything. When people don't practice trustworthiness, sometimes they keep a promise and sometimes they don't. You never know what you can expect of someone who is untrustworthy. When someone cannot be trusted, people become sad and disappointed. If you are not trustworthy, other people never know if they can believe you or count on you.

If you are trustworthy, others can trust you because you keep your word. They don't have to doubt you or check up on you to see if you are doing something you promised to do.

When people are trustworthy with each other, they can relax, knowing that promises will be kept. When people are trustworthy, they can be trusted to tell the truth, to do their part, to give their best. A trustworthy person is the best friend anyone could ever have.

How Do You Practice It?

When you are practicing trustworthiness, you stop and think before making a promise, to be sure it is something you really want to do and that you really can actually do it.

You practice trustworthiness by making a promise to someone or to yourself. Decide to keep your promise rather than just trying to. Start doing what you agreed to do and watch out for things which could prevent you from keeping your agreement. There are traps or obstacles that come along, such as distractions, or feeling too tired, or a job being much harder than you thought it would be.

When you are trustworthy, you keep your word. You keep going, no matter how hard it becomes, because it is very important to you to be worthy of the trust of others.

What would trustworthiness look like if . . .

- Your mother sent you to the store and asked you to bring back the change?

- Your friend told you a secret that he doesn't want anyone else to know?

- You promised to do a chore but start to get distracted by TV or a book?

- Someone asks you to do something that you know in your heart is too hard for you to do?

- You have a daily job to do for your family and you don't feel like doing it?

Signs of Success

Congratulations! You are being trustworthy when you . . .

- Think before you promise something to be sure you can do it

- Remember what you promise others

- Do the things you promise to do

- Keep doing what you promised even when you feel like doing something else

- Let nothing stop you from doing what you said you would do

- Finish doing what you promised to do

Keep trying! You need more practice when you . . .

- Promise something before thinking about it

- Forget what you said you would do

- Promise to do so much that it is impossible to do it all

- Procrastinate—put off starting to do what you promised

- Stop doing what you promised when you feel like doing something else instead

- Keep getting distracted

- Stop before finishing what you promised to do

⊱ *AFFIRMATION* ⊰

I am trustworthy. I keep my promises. I keep my word. I am worthy of the trust others place in me.

⊱ TRUTHFULNESS ⊰

"Then have done with falsehood and speak the truth to each other, for we belong to one another as parts of one body."
—EPHESIANS 4:25

What Is Truthfulness?

Truthfulness means your words and actions are full of truth. Telling the truth means you don't tell lies, even to protect yourself or anyone else. You don't live a lie either. You show people who and what you are without exaggerating to impress them or trying to look like something you are not.

When you are practicing truthfulness, you don't try to believe something you know isn't true. You don't lie to others, and you don't lie to yourself.

Truthfulness is knowing the difference between what is real and what is fantasy. You can have them both, but you do not mix them up. Being true to yourself is living by your true nature, being your true self.

🌱 🌱 🌱

Why Practice Truthfulness?

When people do not practice truthfulness, no one can tell if they are lying or telling the truth. They cannot be trusted to tell the difference between what is true or what is false, what is a story and what really happened. Without trust there is confusion and disunity.

When people practice truthfulness, what they say can be trusted. They say what they mean and mean what they say. Truthfulness builds bonds of love and trust. People know where they stand with an honest and truthful person.

When people investigate the truth for themselves, they don't allow others to dictate their thinking. They don't form prejudices or come to unfair or untrue conclusions. They are people of justice and truth.

How Do You Practice It?

When you practice truthfulness, you choose to tell the truth no matter what. If someone asks you what you think, you tell them what you really think (but tactfully!). When you have made a mistake or done something wrong, you admit it rather than trying to cover it up.

You practice truthfulness by using justice and discernment—recognizing what is true from what is false. If people try to tell you something about another person and you have not seen it with your own eyes, you don't accept it as truth. You investigate the truth for yourself.

You can tell the difference between fantasy and reality, and don't mix them up when you talk to others. If you want to use your imagination, great! It is one of God's gifts. You can make up a story and tell it with great enthusiasm. "I just found diamonds in the garden." Then tell what's really true. "They're really just shiny pebbles." If you catch yourself in the middle of a story, you can always stop and tell what really happened.

You let people see you for who and what you are. You don't exaggerate to look more important. You are valuable just as you are.

What would truthfulness look like if . . .

- Someone tells you that your best friend is saying mean things about you and doesn't want to be your friend anymore?

- You find yourself making up an excuse to cover a mistake?

- You feel like exaggerating how well you did in a game?

- A friend asks you what you think of the six earrings he is wearing?

- Someone makes a comment about all people of a different race?

- You feel like making up a fantastic story to scare your little sister?

Signs of Success

Congratulations! You are practicing truthfulness when you . . .

- Speak only the truth

- Practice justice by investigating the truth for yourself

- Can tell the difference between fact and fantasy

- Say you are telling a story when you make something up

- Admit when you have made a mistake

- Know you are enough—don't exaggerate or deceive to impress others

Keep trying! You need more practice when you . . .

- Accept everything you hear as truth without investigating it for yourself

- Get confused about what is real and what is made up

- Confuse others about what is real and what is fantasy

- Tell lies

- Try to deceive or mislead anyone

- Pretend to be something you are not in order to impress or fool someone

⊰ *AFFIRMATION* ⊱

I am truthful. I speak the truth. I see the truth with my own eyes. I have no need to impress others or exaggerate. I can be my true self.

❧ UNITY ❧

"He who experiences the unity of life, sees his own Self in all beings, and all beings in his own Self, and looks on everything with an impartial eye . . ."

—BHAGAVAD-GITA VI, 29

What Is Unity?

Unity is a very powerful virtue, and it brings great strength. It is a way of seeing the universe as one, designed by the One who created us all. When you practice unity, you allow yourself to feel connected to everything and everyone.

Unity brings harmony, like the music made by the different instruments in an orchestra. Unity doesn't mean to be the same. A flute would never try to sound like a drum. When they are played together, they make beautiful music. When you practice unity, you value what each part brings to the whole. With unity you can strive for harmony with your family at home and your human family around the world.

Unity brings peace. Unity means you don't try to make everyone look, think, act, or talk alike. Through the power of unity you can solve conflict. You can discover a new idea or solution that meets everyone's needs. You can find common ground. Unity is a force so powerful it can light up the world and bring an end to war. With unity you can become a peacemaker wherever you go.

Why Practice Unity?

People of different colors, countries, religions, sexes, and ages are part of one race—the human race. We were all created by God.

Without unity differences scare people and drive them apart. In many parts of the world prejudice causes disunity. People hurt and even kill each other because of differences in their color, their religion, or their ideas. They have forgotten that we are all together on this planet, and that God wants us all to love each other as we are loved.

Without a sense of the unity of all life, people do things that hurt the planet, such as killing animals in a cruel way just to make money from selling their parts, or not being careful with the air and water. Without unity people treat the earth and each other as if they don't matter.

When unity exists in one family, they help each other, listen to each other, and enjoy their different ways of being. Others feel warm and safe being around them. Unity is very powerful, because it is contagious. When one family practices unity, it can spread through the whole world.

How Do You Practice It?

Differences don't have to hurt, whether in a single family or the human family. God loves diversity. It makes life more interesting. Wouldn't the flowers of a garden be dull if they were all the same color? Wouldn't your family be boring if every person were just like you? (Come on. Be honest!)

Unity within a family doesn't mean to act or feel the same. When problems come up, you come together and listen to each person. You find a solution together. You avoid blame. Blame is never a useful starting point for dialogue. You share your feelings and ideas without holding on to them. It's like making soup. You have to drop in your potato to let it flavor the soup. When everyone shares with detachment and trust, the results are wonderful. And everyone can be fed.

When you practice unity, you look at your prejudices and are willing to let them go. Just as every leaf on a tree has a unique design, each person on this earth is someone special. When you practice unity, you try to see the special-ness in every person, not as a reason to be scared or to fight, but as a gift.

When you practice unity, you treat the earth as a sacred home. You are a child of God's universe, and you respect all life within it.

Unity in the human family is feeling how you and others are connected. The joy of one is the joy of all. The hurt of one is the hurt of all. The honor of one is the honor of all.

What would unity look like if . . .

- You see a student in your school who wears a special head dress or clothing in obedience to his religion?

- You notice that all your friends toss their trash into a creek?

- You become angry with a brother or sister and feel like saying hurtful things?

- You overhear someone teasing a child of a different race and calling him names?

- Someone tells you an ethnic joke, and you are tempted to tell it to someone else?

Signs of Success

Congratulations! You are practicing unity when you . . .

- Treat all people as members of one human family

- See the gifts in differences

- Refuse to join in when others express prejudice

- Solve conflict through listening, and finding solutions

- Care for the earth and all living things

- Act like a peacemaker wherever you go

Keep trying! You need more practice when you . . .

- Develop an us-against-them attitude

- Avoid people who are different because you are afraid

- Treat anyone as inferior or better than you are

- Always try to have your own way

- Blame others when they have different points of view

- Abuse the earth or other living things

❧ *AFFIRMATION* ❧

I am a part of God's universe. I appreciate differences. I do not support prejudice. I am a peacemaker. I care for the earth and all living things.

SCRIPTURAL REFERENCES

Baha'i Faith
Selected Writings of Abdu'l-Baha
Writings of Baha'u'llah
Compilations

Buddhism
Dhammapada
Mahavagga

Christianity
Revised English Bible

Hinduism
Bhagavad-Gita

Islam
Al-Qur'an

Judaism
Holy Scriptures

Zoroastrianism
Yasna

⇥ BIBLIOGRAPHY ⇤

Abdu'l-Baha. *Paris Talks*. London: Baha'i Publishing Trust, 1979.

———. *Selections from the Writings of Abdu'l-Baha*. Compiled and published by the Research Department of the Universal House of Justice, Baha'i World Centre, Haifa, Israel, 1978.

Al-Quran, A Contemporary Translation. Ahmed Ali, Princeton: Princeton University Press, 1988.

Baha'i Education: A Compilation. Universal House of Justice. Wilmette, Ill.: National Spiritual Assembly of the Baha'is of the United States, 1977.

Baha'u'llah. *Writings of Baha'u'llah*. New Delhi: National Spiritual Assembly of the Baha'is of India, 1986.

The Bible, Revised English Version. Oxford University Press, Oxford, 1989.

The Dhammapada. Tr. Irving Babbit. New York: New Directions, 1936.

The Geeta. Tr. Shri Purohit Swami (revised edition), London: Faber and Faber Ltd., 1986.

The Holy Scriptures. Philadelphia: Jewish Publication Society of America, 1956.

McCarroll, Tolbert. *Notes from the Song of Life*. Berkeley, Cal.: Celestial Arts, 1987.

Paulus, Trina. *Hope for the Flowers*. New York: Paulist Press, 1972.

The Yasna, in *The Sacred Writings of the World's Great Religions*. Ed. S.E. Frost, Jr. New York: McGraw-Hill, 1972.

APPENDIX A
DISCUSSION EXERCISES

Discussion Exercise 1:
Opposititis—"It Doesn't Matter."

After reading the story of Maria and Robert on page 7, answer these questions, either by group discussion or answer individually and then discuss your answers.

1. What did Maria experience as a child in connection with school and learning?

2. What feelings and needs did she project onto Robert which reflected that experience?

3. What differences were there between Robert's circumstances and Maria's childhood experience?

4. What virtues did Robert need to be called to in this situation?

5. What virtues did Maria need to call on to see Robert's needs distinct from her own?

6. What was the core virtue which Robert seemed attracted to practice?

7. Name a difficulty you experienced in your own childhood which may influence the way you view your children's needs.

8. What was the gift in that difficulty for you? What virtues have you developed as a result?

Suggested answers

1. Inadequacy, shaming by her family, fear
2. Fear of being "dumb," of being found inadequate
3. Robert has not been shamed and he has a home and school environment which supports confidence. Also, he does not have an undiagnosed learning problem as Maria probably did.
4. Excellence, self-discipline, determination
5. Detachment, honesty, trust
6. Excellence
7. and 8. Your call

Discussion Exercise 2:
From Shaming to Naming

Effective ways to support the development of conscience and spiritual growth when children do something unacceptable are:

- Calling them to a virtue
- Giving them a chance to explain their perspective
- Stopping the behavior and giving them a relevant consequence
- When the consequence is served, asking them if they are ready to practice the virtue
- Giving them the opportunity to make reparation
- Acknowledging a virtue when they show an effort to improve

Ways to destroy conscience and stunt spiritual growth in children are:

- Shaming
- Name calling or negative labeling
- Committing verbal abuse
- Beating or hitting
- Overprotecting or excuse making
- Using overly long or punitive consequences
- Ignoring efforts to improve

For each scenario, identify what the parent is doing, using the lists above. Circle the letter of the option which you feel would best support the healthy development of conscience.

1. A thirteen-year-old has come in late after a ground rule has been established for her curfew, including a rule that she should call if unavoidably delayed.
   a. "How could you make me worry like that? Get up to your room, you thoughtless brat! I knew you wouldn't stick to that rule."
   Parent is _____
   b. "Jane, you're late. I was starting to worry when you didn't call. You have always been responsible before. What happened?" (Later

the parent reminds her of the consequence of grounding the next Saturday.)

Parent is _____

c. "Jane, didn't you remember the ground rule? I thought we had an agreement. I'm really disappointed in you. I thought I could trust you."

Parent is _____

2. A three-year-old hits another child on the head with a block. The other child is screaming.

   a. "Mary, it is never okay to hit someone with a weapon. That hurt John badly. Because you didn't play peacefully, go to the other room and stay there until I come to get you."

   Parent is _____

   b. (Slapping Mary's hand) "Bad girl. That's not nice." (Aside to John's mother) "I don't know what's gotten into her today. She's probably just tired."

   Parent is _____

   c. "You could kill someone like that! Get out of here. You're not fit to play with anyone."

   Parent is _____

3. You discover a six-year-old cutting a hole in a good shirt.

   a. "How dare you? Are you crazy? I paid good money for that shirt. You're not getting any more new clothes."

   Parent is _____

   b. (Taking the scissors away) "Shirts aren't for cutting. You need to be responsible with your clothes. Your allowance will have to help pay for the shirt to be replaced."

   Parent is _____

   c. (Grabbing the scissors) "That's it. I've had it. Take down your pants and get ready for a spanking."

   Parent is _____

4. The child in situation 2 who had hit a friend with a block comes back and has played without a problem for fifteen minutes.

a. Parent says nothing—is afraid to make waves.

Parent is _____

b. Parent quietly talks to other parent about the hitting incident and her worries about her daughter's aggressive tendencies.

Parent is _____

c. Parent walks over, smiles and says "You're playing peacefully. Good for you."

Parent is _____

Suggested responses

*Asterisk marks the best response.
1. a. Name calling, verbal abuse, shaming
   *b. Naming the virtue, giving the child a chance to explain, enforcing a consequence
   c. Verbally abusing, shaming
2. *a. Giving relevant consequences, naming the virtue
   b. Hitting, overprotecting
   c. Shaming
3. a. Verbally abusing, shaming
   *b. Naming a virtue, giving a consequence, allowing to make reparation
   c. Shaming, beating
4. a. Ignoring effort
   b. Shaming
   *c. Acknowledging a virtue and effort to improve

Discussion Exercise 3:
Recognize Teachable Moments

Circle the parental response which you consider the most empowering response to a teachable moment. (Choose one.)

1. A four-year-old is having trouble sharing his toys with a visiting child and keeps grabbing them away.
   a. Ask the child which of his toys he is willing to be generous with and which he prefers not to share. Give him a choice within the boundary that when friends come, he must be hospitable.
   b. Tell him he's being selfish, and that if he can't share, his friend will have to go home.
   c. Take the other child into another room.

2. A seven-year-old comes home from school in tears and describes an episode of cruel teasing by other children.
   a. Tell him he has to start standing up for himself. Give him a boxing lesson.
   b. Listen respectfully to his feelings. When he seems finished, ask him what would help him to feel confident and safe at school.
   c. Tell him he should be more detached and if he ignores other kids they will probably stop teasing him.

3. A three-year-old accompanies you on a shopping trip and dismantles a display in a store.
   a. Tell her to be courteous to the store owner and help her put the display back as it was.
   b. Tell her to stop it and to sit down while you put the display back the way it was.
   c. Distract her with a cookie and remember she's just a little girl.

4. You hear your ten-year-old make cruel remarks to one of two friends who are visiting for the afternoon.
   a. In a firm voice, tell him to be nice.

b. Take him into another room and remind him to be kind to his friend.

c. Ignore it. Kids do that.

5. A fourteen-year-old consistently does her chores without having to be reminded.

a. Don't bring it to her attention. She might rebel and stop being so responsible.

b. Tell her she is a good kid and you wish your other children were like her.

c. Tell her you appreciate the reliable way she looks after her responsibilities.

Suggested answers

1.a.; 2.b.; 3.a.; 4.b.; 5.c.

Discussion Exercise 4: Ready or Not

How would you, as caregiver, support your child in the following situations?

(Pick a, b, or c.)

1. A seven-year-old boy in the neighborhood whom you suspect of stealing from the local candy store and who always has lots of money, continually wants to play with your seven-year-old son. Your son is a shy, quiet boy and you're concerned about the influence the other child has on him. Your son is somewhat attracted to this boy and usually wants to play with him.

   a. Forbid your son to play with the child.
   b. Discuss the situation with your son in a frank and honest manner. Then decide whether or not you feel he will lead or follow the other child. If still concerned about the influence, limit or curtail his involvement with the child for a time.
   c. Leave it up to your son. It's his life and he needs to learn to resist temptation.

2. Your 12-year-old daughter wants to stay overnight with a girl whose parents are often away. She is in a somewhat rebellious state lately, and you are concerned she may not admit it if they are to be unsupervised.

   a. Call the parents to find out if they will be home before you give her permission to go for the overnight.
   b. Ask her if the other girl's parents will be home before giving permission.
   c. Tell her no because you cannot be sure the parents will be there.

3. Your nine- and ten-year-old children beg you to let them see a movie which you feel has inappropriate language, violence, or sexual scenes. All their friends have seen it.

   a. You might as well let them. They will feel left out and different if you don't.

b. Explain to them that you don't support violent images going into their memories. Once those images are there, they will stay there forever.

c. Try to convince them it is wrong to see it, but leave the choice up to them.

4. You live in a neighborhood in which some children have been picked up by drivers and molested.

a. Make sure you drive your children everywhere, even around the block.

b. Keep the children in the house and don't mention anything. It will upset them too much.

c. Explain to your children that some people hurt children and that to keep them safe, they may not wander in the neighborhood alone. Set a new ground rule that they must be accompanied by you or an older sibling. Explain about saying "no" to strangers.

5. Your toddler is with you while you visit a friend. Her child is irritable and aggressive. You see your two-year-old starting to become edgy and upset.

a. Tell the children to play nicely.

b. Either engage the children in a story or other calming activity or take your child home.

c. Ask your friend to control her child better.

Suggested answers

1.b.; 2.a.; 3.b.; 4.c.; 5.b.

Discussion Exercise 5:
Virtues Acknowledgments

In the following situations, which virtues do you think apply? How would you acknowledge the child?

Example: After receiving a consequence of a five-minute time out for hitting her brother, Marla has returned and apologized. Her father notices she has been playing peacefully for about five minutes. Smiling at her, he says, "Marla, I see you're remembering to be peaceful with your brother."

An effective virtues acknowledgment has three parts: (1) an opening phrase: "Marla, I see you're remembering to be . . ." (2) a virtue: "peaceful . . ." (3) the specific way it is being practiced: "with your brother."

1. Your eight-year-old son has started piano lessons and is grumbling about having to practice but does so without having to be reminded for three days in a row. What virtues could you acknowledge? What would you say?

2. Your three-year-old touches the baby softly. What virtues could you name? What would you say?

3. A five-year-old is reluctant to leave a television show to set the table, but does come to do it. What virtue could you acknowledge? What would you say?

4. A ten-year-old has had to wait for half an hour while you finish a task. What virtue could you acknowledge? What would you say?

Suggested virtues

1. Excellence, steadfastness, self-discipline
2. Gentleness, caring, love
3. Reliability, trustworthiness, helpfulness, detachment
4. Patience

Discussion Exercise 6:
Virtues Corrections

Here are some common situations in which parents have the opportunity to call the child to the virtues. It is much more supportive of the child as a spiritual being, since criticism and name-calling are avoided and the virtue is the focus of attention.

Example: A father sees his four-year-old son starting to get upset while playing with some other children. It looks like block throwing could begin any second. Father has the choice to preach: "Calm down, Peter, or you'll have to leave"; to ignore it and hope things improve, or to act preventively and teach a virtue at the same time. For example, taking the child on his lap gently, he asks, "Peter, do you feel you can play peacefully now or do you need to play by yourself for a while?"

What virtues apply in these situations and what might you say to the child?

1. A ten-year-old has borrowed some tools and left them in the yard.

_____

_____

2. A three-year-old has gotten into mother's drawer and started to use lipstick to decorate the wall.

_____

_____

3. An eight-year-old has worn the same clothes for three days.

_____

_____

4. A six-year-old is screaming at a brother or sister and brandishing a large stick.

_____

_____

Answers
1. Trustworthiness, responsibility, reliability
2. Respect for others' things and for the house
3. Cleanliness
4. Peacefulness

Discussion Exercise 7:
The Power of Consistency

Read the following true story and then answer the questions below.

A family has two boys ages six and eight, who are permitted to explore the woods near their house and have the freedom of the neighborhood when together, with the ground rule that they be home by 5:00 P.M. Not 5:05, not 5:03, but 5:00. They had never broken this rule.

One day, at 4:58, their mother was worried, since they had never been this late, usually coming in at least ten minutes before curfew. On the dot of 5:00, the front door flew open and two little boys landed with a thud, face down, covered with brambles and burrs. "Did we make it?" they gasped desperately. "We were lost in the woods." "Just in the nick of time, fortunately for you. Good obedience, boys," Mom replied.

What was the dreaded consequence had they broken the ground rule? They would have lost their freedom to roam the neighborhood and would have had to stay in the house the next day.

What do you think held such power in these children's minds?

_____

_____

Why was the ground rule so important to them?

_____

_____

How did having the rule keep the parent free from getting into a power struggle?

_____

_____

What difference did the parent's consistency and exactness make in this instance?

_____

_____

In your opinion, how did successful adherence to the ground rule affect these children's self-esteem?

_____

_____

It is unlikely that the strong motivation for keeping this rule came from fear of the terrors of staying home for a day. Having a rule meant something to these children. It was their limit and in their own way, they cherished it. They probably wanted to keep their perfect record. The parent's absolute consistency was something they could always count on without fail.

Discussion Exercise 8:
What Difference Can a Ground Rule Make?

The following exercise is designed to help you look at the differences which can occur in the presence or absence of ground rules.

What distinction do you see between these two scenarios in which a 13-year-old who usually cleans his room on Saturday mornings instead rushes out to go to a sports practice?:

1. In this scenario, no actual ground rule has been set. There is an unspoken expectation that rooms should be cleaned every Saturday.

PARENT: Jeff, get in your room and clean it up now! I don't care if you're late for practice. Do as I say or you'll be grounded for a month!
How is this parent coming across?

_____

_____

How is the parent actually feeling? In control or helpless?

_____

_____

How is Jeff likely to respond to this command?

_____

_____

How does the absence of a ground rule invite a power struggle?

_____

_____

In the absence of clear ground rules, the parent can come across as an arbitrary, angry authority, inviting rebellion. A parent is likely to feel challenged, particularly by an adolescent who becomes defiant. This leads to power struggles where a youngster like Jeff may get so angry that he does rebel, runs out of the house and leaves the parent feeling helpless and angry. This accelerates the need for power moves on the parent's part to reassert authority.

2. A family ground rule has been established that each Saturday, rooms must be clean before anyone leaves the house, or by noon at the latest.

JEFF: *(rushes up to Dad and says)* I can't clean my room. I'm late for practice.
DAD: Jeff, as soon as you have cleaned your room, you can go. You know the ground rule.

How is Jeff likely to respond?

_____

_____

Would the parent feel tempted to lecture and nag? ("Jeff, you know very well it's a ground rule. Now get in there and do it!")

_____

_____

What is likely to occur if the parent calmly stated the situation as above, knowing that the ground rule is clear and that Jeff is aware of it?

_____

_____

What is the best way to deal with pleading and bargaining? ("But, Dad, I'll be late and I'm quarterback. The coach will get mad if I'm late. I promise to clean it when I get back.")

_____

_____

290

In this example of a common, every-day occurrence, the parent has an important choice: to be a dictator, nag, indulger . . . or educator. There are many times which call for flexibility on a parent's part. However, when it comes to a ground rule, it is better for the parent to remain consistent. Jeff had a choice to get up earlier to clean his room, knowing that he would not be allowed out until it was clean. He could have been creative and cleaned it Friday afternoon.

This is a clear, simple, agreed upon rule which he knew about. In the face of bargaining, a parent simply says "You know the rule." If there is a really good reason why changes need to be made to a rule, a child should have the right to bring it up for discussion, but not as a quick, momentary thing when it is inconvenient to follow it.

What is a child likely to learn when ground rules are simple, fair, clear, and consistent?

_____

_____

How is Jeff likely to respond to other ground rules based on how this one is handled?

_____

_____

How would his respect for other family ground rules be effected if this one is ignored?

_____

_____

When ground rules are consistent and non-negotiable, children learn trust. They can count on the limits as limits. If one ground rule is bent or broken, then a child sees that others may be broken and every rule is up for negotiation, challenge, or wheedling.

The beauty of using ground rules is that children and parents are not pitted against each other in power struggles. The rules speak for themselves.

Discussion Exercise 9:
Give Choices Within Boundaries

1. Bedtime Blues

A mother who has set a ground rule of 7:30 bedtime asks her three-year-old, "Do you want to go to bed now? You must be sleepy."

a.   What's wrong with this approach?

_____

_____

b.   What is likely to be the child's response?

_____

_____

c. Suggest how you would offer this child a choice within the ground rule of a 7:30 bedtime.

_____

_____

Suggested responses

a. Parent is giving a choice where she has already decided there is no choice. It is a setup for a power struggle.
b. To want to stay up.
c. "Do you want to wear your blue pajamas or red ones?" "Do you want Dad or Mom to do story and prayers tonight?"

2. Preventing Disaster

While visiting Aunt Ann with her mother, a baby is getting closer to a fragile vase, looking over her shoulder at mother to see what she will do.

Please rate the following responses as

(M) Most effective

(L) Least effective

(S) Somewhat effective

Identify what boundary the parent is setting in each option and discuss the reasons for your ratings.

_____ a. In a challenging tone, mother says "No. No, Sara. Don't you dare. If you do, I'll spank you."

Parent is _____

_____ b. Calmly mother says, "That vase is not for touching, Sara. Be respectful of Auntie Ann's belongings. Here's something you can play with."

Parent is _____

_____ c. The baby continues to touch every breakable thing left out in Aunt Ann's living room, and mother decides she is not ready to handle all that glittering temptation. Mother decides to redirect her natural curiosity by relocating to the kitchen.

Parent is _____

Suggested responses

a. Least effective. Parent is threatening. Expecting the worst of the child leads her to do it.

b. Most effective. Parent is offering an acceptable choice. Gives child best opportunity to develop self-discipline and respect.

c. Somewhat effective. Mother realizes this is more than the baby can handle. Is positively redirecting her.

3. Power Plays

Read these examples of different ways a parent can handle a potential power struggle, in which a toddler has been sitting on a dining room chair waiting for a dinner guest to arrive. Then answer the questions below each example:

3a. The Battle of Wills

MOMMY: Chuckie, our dinner guest is here. Wouldn't you like to move out of the big chair and into your high chair?
CHUCKIE: Nope.
MOMMY: Chuckie, if you don't, Mr. K. will have nowhere to sit.
CHUCKIE: Uh-uh.
MOMMY: Chuckie, won't you be more comfy in your own chair so you can see everyone?
(Chuckie is unmoved.)

      a. Why is this a losing battle for the parent? What has she neglected to do?

      _____

      _____

      b. How could this situation be changed by the way the parent "frames" it for the child? Which choices, if any, do you think Chuckie should have?

      _____

      _____

Suggested responses

      a. She has set this up to give Chuckie a choice when in her mind there is no choice. She has neglected to set boundaries around the choices.
      b. She can give Chuckie choices within whatever condition is acceptable to her.

3b. From Tyranny to Obedience

Here's how a Virtues-based approach might go, with the goal of teaching Chuckie obedience and courtesy.

MOMMY: Chuckie, it's time to move into your own chair now. Mr. K. is here.
CHUCKIE: No, I don't want to.

MOMMY: *(picking Chuckie up and putting him in his high chair)* Wouldn't Mr. K. look silly in your high chair?

Chuckie would probably get a chuckle out of this but would also know his mom meant business. Should he be in a rebellious mood (or missed his nap), he may accelerate the struggle.

CHUCKIE: I don't wanna!
MOMMY: Chuck, you have a choice now. You can be obedient and join us for dinner or have dinner in your room.

    a. What differences do you see in the mother's attitude from Example 3a to Example 3b?

_____

_____

    b. What other differences do you see between these two examples?

_____

_____

    c. How do you think Chuckie might feel about himself (unconsciously or consciously) if allowed to get the upper hand with his mother?

_____

_____

Suggested responses

    a. In Example 3a, mother is unsuccessfully manipulative and feels helpless. She has set up a power struggle. In Example 3b, she is firm, loving, and giving Chuckie a clear choice within boundaries.
    b. No boundaries vs. boundaries; power struggle set-up vs. none; supportive of Chuckie's selfishness vs. his courtesy.
    c. Outwardly smug while inwardly feeling anxious, uncertain, guilty.

3c. Creative Flexibility

Chuckie stays in the big chair when Mr. K. walks in. Chuckie doesn't want to sit in his high chair.

MOTHER: Chuckie. You may sit in a big chair tonight if you will help your dad get a chair for Mr. K. Why don't you ask Mr. K. where he wants you to put his chair.

a. In your opinion, what is this teaching Chuckie?

_____

_____

b. Is this an approach with which you would be comfortable? Why or why not?

_____

_____

4. Choice Time

Read and discuss the following example of giving a child choices within boundaries:

Two women have arranged to meet in a park when one comes to town after being away for two years. They are close friends and very eager to talk. One has three small children including a clingy two-year-old. The two-year-old starts fussing and trying to get her mother's attention just as the two friends launch into the long-awaited conversation. Mom excuses herself, goes off a little distance, and takes Maria on her lap. "Maria, it's choice time. You have two choices now in being courteous. I want to talk to my friend. We need to hear each other. You can either sit quietly in my lap, or play with your trucks over there with Carlos and Luis. Which do you choose?"

Maria chose to play with her brothers, secure that if she needed a hug she could do so on the condition that she did it quietly.

a. What virtues were involved here?

_____

_____

b. How did the mother model the virtues?

_____

_____

c. Name three reasons why this approach worked for Maria and her mother.

_____

_____

_____

Suggested responses

a. Courtesy, obedience, patience.
b. She was courteous by speaking to Maria privately.
c. Maria had two acceptable choices. Mother was clear. Mother was taking care of her own needs as well as Maria's. Maria's dignity was not upset by the obedience her mother expected.

Discussion Exercise 10:
What's Wrong with This Picture?

a. Discuss the *effect* these parental behaviors would have on a child who is learning about the virtues.

b. Then state what *actions* or *words* would be a good substitute in each of these situations.

c. Name the *virtues* involved in each case.

1. The children are playing loudly in the playroom when Dad is trying to rest. "Stop that yelling!" screamed Dad as he grew red in the face.

   a. _____

   _____

   b. _____

   _____

   c. _____

   _____

2. "Don't hit your little sister!" yelled Mother as she slapped her son's bottom.

   a. _____

   _____

   b. _____

   _____

   c. _____

   _____

3. "I know I'm an hour late," puffed Mom as she rushed in from a long day of work. "Why haven't you taken the garbage out yet? Can't I rely on you for anything?"

   a. _____

   _____

   b. _____

   _____

   c. _____

   _____

4. "Did you take Jimmy's truck?" Dad asks, knowing his daughter is hiding her brother's toy behind her back.

   a. _____

   _____

   b. _____

   _____

   c. _____

   _____

Suggested answers

1. a. Courtesy is being skirted. Dad is modeling loss of self-control—yelling for yelling. Child would feel shamed.
   b. "I'm trying to rest. I need quiet. Please be thoughtful and keep things quiet for the next hour."
   c. Courtesy, helpfulness, thoughtfulness.

2. a. Mother is modeling violence at the same time as telling the child not to be violent. There is no learning other than not to make mother angry. Child would feel shamed.

b. "Be peaceful with your sister. If you're angry, use your voice to tell her."

c. Peacefulness, gentleness, assertiveness.

3. a. Mother is preaching reliability when she has just had a lapse in reliability herself. It is a confusing time for the children to hear about the virtue. Mother is also not being loving or peaceful in her first contact with the children that evening. It has set a tone of tension.

b. "I apologize for being late. It was unavoidable." Later, she can talk to the children about needing to remember the garbage.

c. Reliability, peacefulness, humility.

4. a. The father is being dishonest in asking a question as if he doesn't know the answer. He is being manipulative and setting up a power struggle. If you know the answer, don't ask the question!

b. While holding out his hand for the truck, "When you take Jimmy's truck without asking, it is disrespectful. Be respectful of his things, and maybe when he's ready, he will share."

c. Honesty, respect.

Discussion Exercise 11:
A Family Values History

Forming Values Is a Spiritual Activity

As creators of the culture in your home, as the architects of your family values, you have enormous influence in your children's lives. A code of values is an important part of spirituality. Values vary from family to family, but they are always present. Whether the family places value on being an efficient thief after three generations of thievery or are working for world peace, children will pick up those values as their own. The values we acquire over the years, particularly in childhood, continually determine our choices as adults. They become the content of our personal code of ethics. They help us act responsibly or irresponsibly. They give our lives meaning and purpose. The process of growing up is one of integrating our values. This integration is truly an exercise in spirituality.

The purpose of the following exercise is to help you identify the values your parents passed on to you, how you feel about those values as an adult, and to reflect on the values you wish to pass on to your children. Use additional paper for lengthier answers!

Give a Brief History of Your Original Family Culture

1. When you were a child, what were some of the values your parents transmitted to you? What was most important in your family? How did you know? (For example: Was leisure important? Education? Family ties? Religion?) Are there any pet phrases or "sayings" you remember?

_____

_____

2. What were the values of your family when it came to saving or spending money?

_____

_____

3. How were your family's material and spiritual values passed on to you? What do you remember your parents talking about most?

_____

_____

4. What place did God and religion have in your life as a family? How has that affected your religious practices as they are now?

_____

_____

5. Pick three words that capture the values your family cared about most.

_____

_____

6. Which of the values of your family of origin do you want to pass on to your children? What values do you want to change or add?

_____

_____

Discussion Exercise 12:
A Confidence History

Acting Responsibly Is a Spiritual Activity

From the time they are very young, children can develop a strong sense of responsibility and the self-esteem that goes with it, simply by being treated as if they are responsible.

When God places a capacity within us, it needs to be tapped. Children are capable when they are very young of being responsible for their belongings, being counted on as valuable members of the family team, and making their own choices. Failing to honor this capacity as it emerges is one of the worst forms of parental negligence.

When we encourage children to act responsibly, we are giving them the opportunity to exercise their spirituality. Making choices and taking responsibility are daily acts. They provide many teachable moments. They are also a primary means for a child to develop self-esteem and self-confidence.

One of the best ways for children to acquire self-confidence is to receive moral support from parents and other caregivers when they try something new, particularly a task to be accomplished or a problem to be solved. The most empowering support comes as enthusiastic acknowledgment for effort and success, and gentle encouragement to keep trying when mistakes occur.

The worst way to learn confidence and responsibility is to be criticized, attacked, pampered, teased, left out of meaningful work, or ignored.

To understand what your children need from you, recall these issues in light of your own experience as a child.

Visualize yourself as a child and write some of the things you learned in regard to self-confidence and responsibility. Use a separate piece of paper if needed.

1. Do you remember what it was like for you in learning to read, tie your shoelaces, ride a bike, drive a car, cook a meal? Did you generally have the feeling that your parents considered you competent?

_____

_____

2. Negatives are often said with much emotion, while positives are minimized. Which do you recall most clearly: negative or positive responses from your parents or the other significant adults in your world?

_____

_____

3. What were some of the "labels" your parents used about you and how have they affected you?

_____

_____

4. Which of your qualities or virtues did your parents most appreciate and respect?

_____

_____

5. What insights have you gained about parenting your children through these reflections on your own upbringing?

_____

_____

Discussion Exercise 13:
Spiritual Companioning with Children

Spiritual companioning would serve any human being when confronted with a moral decision. Beginning when children are small gives them a wonderful head start in their spiritual growth and self-esteem.

In the following exercise, please bear in mind that the listening part might take quite some time and would require a good deal of respectful and attentive silence on the parent's part.

In the following situations, write:

a. A typical response most parents would give in this situation
b. A question with which a parent could begin to help the child empty her cup in order to support her toward her own clarity.
c. A virtues reflection question to help the child resolve the issue.

Example: A nine-year-old has spent all her time with another neighborhood child. A new girl has moved into the neighborhood and is vying for her attention. She feels confused about whether to give up her old friend for a new one.

Questions a parent might ask (with lots of listening in between):

Cup-emptying question: "What do you feel the most confused about, Lin?"
Virtues reflection question: "What do you feel would be fair to both girls?"

1. A child your son doesn't like keeps calling and coming to the door to play. Your son comes to you to ask what to do.

   a. Typical response: _____

   _____

   b. Cup-emptying question: _____

   _____

   c. Virtues reflection question: _____

   _____

2. Your ten-year-old daughter complains that your twelve-year-old daughter and she have an agreement of sharing clothes but lately her sister is borrowing her favorite things all the time, and she wants you to stop it.

    a. Typical response: _____

    _____

    b. Cup-emptying question: _____

    _____

    c. Virtues reflection question: _____

    _____

3. Your seven-year-old child comes to you very upset after "catching" a friend in the act of stealing from a local store. She doesn't know whether to tell the store owner, the child's parents, or just ignore it.

    a. Typical response: _____

    _____

    b. Cup-emptying question: _____

    _____

    c. Virtues reflection question: _____

    _____

4. Your five-year-old comes home and tells you an elaborate story which you know he has made up.

    a. Typical response: _____

    _____

    b. Cup-emptying question: _____

    _____

    c. Virtues reflection question: _____

    _____

5. Your eight-year-old bursts into the house and confesses he has just stolen a candy bar from the local grocery store. It is still unopened. In his confession, he tells you he was just curious about whether or not he could do it without being caught.

   a. Typical response: _____

   _____

   b. Cup-emptying question: _____

   _____

   c. Virtues reflection question: _____

   _____

Suggested answers

1. a. "Why don't you just let him play?"
   b. "What bothers you about playing with him?"
      "What are you uncomfortable about in saying 'no' to him?"
   c. "How can you be honest and tactful with him? What would give you the courage to do it?"

2. a. "I'll talk to her about it."
   b. "What bothers you most about the way this is going?"
      "What feels unfair about your agreement?"
   c. "What would be an honorable way to change your agreement?"

3. a. "I don't want you playing with her anymore."
   b. "What worries you about this?"
   c. "What do you think would be most helpful to your friend?"

4. a. "Don't make up stories."
   b. "It's fun to make things up. What happens next?"
   c. "What's truthful? Tell me what really happened."

5. a. "What got into you? Go back and tell the store owner what you did."
   b. "What were you curious about?"
      "How do you feel about taking the candy?"
   c. "What do you need to do to make it right? What would be honest?"

When moral decisions are at stake, you want to give children the opportunity to make good decisions to the extent that they are capable. If they are unable to decide, it is all right to advise them, but to the extent that the decision comes from them, their spiritual growth and their self-esteem will increase.

APPENDIX B

The Do's and Don'ts of Bringing Out the Best in Our Children and Ourselves

What follows is an outline of the first three chapters, summarizing the Do's and Don'ts of spiritual parenting.

Chapter 1: Who Are Our Children, Really?

In serving as your child's mentor:

Do	Don't
Look for the virtues in yourself and your children	Be a perfectionist
See a child as a spiritual champion	Indulge or overprotect a child
Be an educator	Be merely a caretaker
Focus on moral readiness	See your child as a blank slate
Steward your child's innate virtues	Leave your child to his own devices
Guide your child to act on the best within	See your child as just a reflection on you
	Treat your child as a little prince or princess

In seeing your children as they really are:

Do	Don't
See your child as an independent spiritual being	Take all the responsibility for your children's choices

Do

Be discerning about what your children truly need

Expect excellence

Appreciate your child's unique style of being

Set clear boundaries about your expectations

Be tolerant when a child is having an off day

Give your child lots of non-compulsory time

Know when to get out of the way

Don't

Fall into the opposititis trap

Give children too much of what you didn't have

Overpraise children

Impose your own style as a value

Impose unrealistic expectations

Expect your child to make up for your lacks

Teach all the time

Chapter 2: What's a Parent to Do?

As an Educator

Strategy 1: Recognize Teachable Moments

Do

Realize that life is for learning our lessons

See tests as opportunities to hone virtues

Tap into the child's innate virtues

Name virtues

Call children to specific virtues they need to practice

Use virtues, not labels

Catch children in the act of committing virtues

Do for children what they cannot do for themselves

See guilt as a signal for change

Don't

Ignore teachable moments

Avoid life's challenges

Manage behavior

Shame and blame

Label children with negative words or virtues

Do for children what they can do for themselves

Abuse guilt by shaming a child for mistakes

When your child does something really terrible:

Do

Stop the behavior
Name a specific virtue
Explain briefly how it's wrong
Give an immediate consequence
Encourage the child to make
    reparation
Be a teacher, not a preacher

Don't

Slip into shaming
Be shocked or surprised
Use the virtues to moralize
Lecture
Should on children

Strategy 2: Speak the Language of the Virtues

Do

Use virtues to acknowledge
Use virtues to correct behavior
Create your family vision by
    choosing your core virtues
Look for ways to be of service as
    a family
Use moderation with
    acknowledgments
Always acknowledge effort
Be specific when using virtues to
    correct
Name the act, not the actor
Make simple, positive requests
Be specific and accurate

Don't

Use shaming, blaming, framing
    language
Mislabel children's natural tendencies
    as negative
Constantly acknowledge every
    positive thing
Breed overdependence on praise
Worry that praise will create a big ego
Give vague instructions like "Stop
    that."
Insult the child's character
Say "You never"
Encourage people-pleasing

As an Authority

Strategy 3: Set Clear Boundaries

The healthy use of authority:

Do

Use authority in service of a child's learning

Provide reasonable parental authority

Set clear boundaries

Distinguish between what is negotiable and what is non-negotiable

Be an educator who can sometimes be a pal

Be a responsible leader

Give children predictable routines and rituals

Don't

Be ambivalent about using your authority

Be too permissive

Be too strict or dominant

Be too democratic

Negotiate everything

Deprive children of order and predictability

Slide back and forth on a wave of guilt

Expect children to like and approve everything you do

In establishing family ground rules:

Do

Be moderate; have five or six rules

Be specific to the needs of your family

Be positive. Base ground rules on virtues.

Establish specific, relevant consequences ahead of time

Let the punishment fit the crime

Give educative consequences

Establish restorative justice

Be consistent

Communicate the rules clearly

Make sure children understand what a consequence is for

Don't

Overcomplicate the rules

Express ground rules in the negative (e.g. no hitting)

Dictate the consequence by your irritation level

Give punitive consequences

Use retributive justice

Be inconsistent in enforcing the rules

Keep the rules only in your own mind

Give second chances when it comes to ground rules

Keep the same rules too long

Give small children too many open choices

Do	**Don't**
Listen to feelings	Argue when boundaries are being violated
Make the ground rules nonnegotiable	
Be flexible by changing the rules as children grow older	
Give choices within boundaries	
Set boundaries when respect is violated	
Set boundaries to prepare children for new situations	

In your approach to discipline:

Do	**Don't**
Link freedom to responsibility	Feed conflict
Reward children for abiding by the boundaries consistently	Yell at children continually
Require simple obedience when it comes to safety	Be too passive with children
Use a commanding voice when safety is involved	Bicker constantly
Prevent power struggles	
Always acknowledge effort and improvement	

As a Guide

Strategy 4: Honor the Spirit

Do	**Don't**
Share your knowledge and your skills	Ignore opportunities for children to learn new skills
Give children responsibilities they can handle	Ignore the need for reverence
	Cross talk during sharing circles

Do	**Don't**
Share your family stories	Neglect the importance of special
Listen to your children's stories	times
Create routines of reverence	
Hold sharing circles	
Mark special times with special rituals	

If God is part of your beliefs:

Do	**Don't**
Start early to mention the Creator	Wait until children are older
Mention God in the normal course of daily life	Expect faith to develop
Show children your thankfulness and reverence	Reserve spirituality for worship services
Engage your children in spiritual practices	
Pray with your children	
Encourage meditation	
Attend worship services	
Experience reverence for nature	
Share your child's natural sense of wonder	

As a Counselor

Strategy 5: Offer the Art of Spiritual Companioning

Do	**Don't**
See a child as a whole, complete person	Try to do a child's spiritual work for her
Offer compassion and detachment	Sympathize

Do	**Don't**
Trust the child's process	Take on a child's feelings as your responsibility
Be present to your child's feelings	Suppress feelings in the name of virtue
Take children seriously	
Listen to feelings after a child has paid his consequence	Preach at a child when he has paid his consequence
Help a child to make her own moral choices	Give advice or rescue when a child has a moral choice
Ask door-opening questions	Second-guess children
Offer receptive silence	Fill every silence
Ask cup-emptying questions	Rush to find solutions
Ask what and how	Ask who or why
Focus on sensory cues (vision, hearing, feeling)	Minimize or distract when a child is injured
Ask questions which help children to reflect on the virtues involved	Preempt the child's resolution of moral dilemmas
Ask closure and integration questions	Have an agenda for how a child is to resolve the issue
Give relevant virtues acknowledgments	Give a virtues label instead of an acknowledgment

Chapter 3: How to Apply
The Family Virtues Guide in Your Family

Do	**Don't**
Apply *The Family Virtues Guide* to personal and spiritual growth of everyone in the family	Use *The Family Virtues Guide* to manipulate behavior
Model realness and honesty	Let meetings go long even if they are going well
Set a time for your first meeting	Cram family business into virtues meetings
Practice moderation in length of meetings	Focus on behavior that needs correcting
Choose a simple format	

Do

Be orderly
Be creative
Have fun
Keep it positive
Keep it simple and sacred
Set boundaries for sharing circles
Play virtues games
Use art and music
Use opening and closing rituals
Act with tact—give
    acknowledgment, correction,
    and thanks
Be a spiritual companion

Don't

Treat a family virtues meeting too
    casually
Treat a family virtues meeting too
    seriously
Let the meeting be boring
Just get together any time
Reprimand each other for failing to
    practice the virtue
Give lectures

❧ APPENDIX C ❦
HOW TO MAKE A
VIRTUES TREE FELT BOARD

Having a homemade felt board to which you can attach a felt tree and felt fruits will enable you to do all kinds of fun activities around the virtues as the "Fruits of Human Life."

Equipment needed

- Cardboard (section of medium cardboard box, for example)
- Piece of blue or pale color felt to paste to cardboard
- Glue or paste
- Small squares of felt in varied colors
- Large squares of brown and green felt for trunk and top of tree
- Scissors

Instructions

1. Paste a large piece of felt onto cardboard to make your felt board.
2. Engage children in cutting out different shapes of fruits to go with the colors of felt you have as well as the tree itself.
3. Cut out a tree trunk.
4. Cut out a leafy top.
5. Cut out fruits such as:

Obedient Orange	*Kind Kiwi*	*Trustworthy Turnip*
Peaceful Peach	*Prayerful Pear*	*(okay, it's a veggie)*
Reverent Raisin	*Tactful Tomato*	*Courteous Kumquat*
Generous Grape		

You get the idea . . .

Have the children draw faces on them. You can add a fruit each week or do some all at once.

Children enjoy playing with this felt board, and it can be used to make up stories, acknowledge efforts, and any number of creative applications.

❧⊁ APPENDIX D ⊱❧

PROGRAMS AND MATERIALS
OF THE VIRTUES PROJECT

The Virtues Project offers a wide range of programs and materials for people seeking to deepen their spiritual practices; parents raising morally conscious children; schools creating a culture of character; caregivers seeking to address the spiritual dimension; organizations seeking to enhance corporate spirit.

The Programs of The Virtues Project include:

- Conference presentations by Linda Kavelin Popov and Dan Popov, Ph.D.
- Virtues Project Facilitator Intensives in many countries
- Workshops for Parents, Schools, Corporations, and Social Service Agencies
- Organizational Consulting
- Spiritual Growth Intensives for Individuals
- Community Development and Healing Projects

The Virtues Project materials include:

Virtues Reminders: Cards describing the virtues, used in "Virtues Picks"
Wallet Cards of the 52 virtues in *The Family Virtues Guide*
Poster, "Virtues: The Gifts Within" full color 24" x 36"
Audio Tapes

World Wide Web Site http://www.virtuesproject.com
Visit our website

- To view a catalogue of materials and how to order them
- To peruse our global newsletter

- To obtain a schedule of all presentations, workshops, and trainings
- To find the location of Virtues Project Associations and facilitators

To order materials in the United States and Canada call (888) 261-5611; from outside North America call (423) 870-3884; or e-mail us about Programs and Materials at virtuespro@aol.com.

The authors of *The Family Virtues Guide* are (left to right) Linda Kavelin Popov, Dan Popov, Ph.D., and John Kavelin, co-founders of The Virtues Project.

Linda Kavelin Popov is President of The Virtues Project, Inc. She is a psychotherapist, organizational consultant, former hospice spiritual care director, and mother. She facilitates community healing and development throughout the world and speaks internationally on the cultivation of personal and corporate virtues.

Dan Popov, Ph.D. is a pediatric clinical psychologist, a community developer and corporate consultant. He is the Executive Director of WellSpring International Educational Foundation which develops and distributes multi-faith spiritual education materials. He is a scholar in the sacred texts of the world's religions.

John H. Kavelin is a designer and Senior Show Producer with Walt Disney Imagineering. He is a director for The Virtues Project, Inc. He played a key role in the founding and development of The Virtues Project.